HOPE FOUND IN PARADISE LOST

God's pathway to freedom, joy,
and triumphant living

LuAnn Grambow

PRESS

Urs Urs,

I know the cover of this book looks pretty dull, but the book is far from it. I've been reading this book to process my life history + see what is it that keeps me from complete freedom in Christ.

I hope that you will read it + process the same! I couldn't go w/o sharing it! We ♡ you,

Cena + Stephen

"Now the Lord is the Spirit, and where the Spirit of the Lord is there is freedom. And we who with unveiled faces all reflect the Lord's glory, are being transformed into His likeness with ever-increasing glory, which comes from the Lord, who is the Spirit." 2 Corinthians 3:17, 18

"Consider it pure joy, my brothers, whenever you face trials of many kinds, because you know that the testing of your faith develops perseverance. Perseverance must finish its work so that you may be mature and complete, not lacking anything." James 1:2-4

CHAPTERS

Foreword

There are some people who believe that if you walk closely with God, your spouse will never get sick, you will never lose your job, and your children will not mess with drugs. Those who believe this are not living in the world described in the Bible. The fact is Christians have automobile accidents, their houses get infested with termites, and many Christians die young.

If one believes that the Christian life is always beautiful, then when crises come, one will likely lash out at God. "How could you let this happen to me?" "If you really loved me, You would heal my child." In short, we often feel good about God when things are going well and mad at God (or at least confused) when trouble comes.

We might dismiss the matter by saying that these people have a non-biblical view of God. I believe it is more serious than that. It is highly possible that these people are idol worshippers. They are trusting in health, relationships, good jobs, and material comforts to bring them satisfaction and happiness, instead of trusting in God who will be there when all of these things are gone.

In Hope Found in Paradise Lost, LuAnn Grambow presents a metaphor which I think many people will find helpful.

The walls we build to protect ourselves from hurt, often are barriers to our spiritual growth. When a crisis comes, the walls fall down around us and we stand helpless. It is in our need that we often encounter God in a whole new way. In the Old Testament, Job speaks to God and indicates that before his troubles, "my ears had heard of you." After the crises he said, "Now my eyes have seen you."

This book does not offer a quick fix to the pains of life. However, it does draw out the roadmap whereby you can overcome your enslavement to the pursuit of comfortable life circumstances, come to really know God, and let Him change you into someone whom He can use to bless the world. To be used of God to accomplish His purposes in your generation – there is no higher calling.

Gary D. Chapman, Ph.D.
Author of The Five Love Languages and The Five Languages of Apology

HOPE LOST

B efore profound loss occurs we can skip blithely through life, naively believing that we can make all our dreams come true-that we can achieve a Paradise-like life experience. But loss is a multi-faceted enemy of the soul of mankind. It can come suddenly, in a moment of time, or gradually, catching us unaware and unprepared when its stealthy approach reaches our unguarded heart. It can be loss of a concrete reality in our lives, or loss of an abstract-a dream, a necessary belief, a sacred purpose.

It comes as a phone call in the night telling that a loved one has died. It comes as a still, small voice telling you your aging body will never have vitality again. It comes as the screeching of tires and brakes as metal collides with flesh with deathly results. It comes as the boss, behind closed doors, telling you your job is being eliminated. It comes as a marriage partner announcing he doesn't love you anymore and is leaving. It comes as a gradual realization that the dreamed-of career achievements will never be. It comes as a phone call from someone claiming to be your partners' love interest. It comes as you realize your financial ruin is unavoidable and you will lose everything. It comes as a doctor's solemn, sad announcement of a terminal disease. It comes as premature labor pains that give birth to death and disabling grief. It comes as a violent attack that shatters your body and unbalances your psyche. The list is as endless as the myriad unwelcome, unwanted, and sometimes catastrophic circumstances that life can bring our way. Whatever form it takes, loss leaves a devastated soul in its wake, struggling to survive, clinging to hope even as it fades away. Life makes no sense anymore, has no goals worth pursuing, is painful without remedy. Paradise becomes Paradise Lost; life becomes hopeless. Satan celebrates while God orchestrates. Suffering is claimed to be the measure of our character as well as the cultivator of it. How do we survive, let alone allow God to use loss as a refining fire in our lives?

That question consumed my life when loss came uninvited to my door. My catapulted entrance to Paradise Lost began on a fresh, shimmery spring morning when everything in my "Paradise recreated" world seemed to be perfectly in place. My husband of 21 years said to me, "Let's go for a walk." Those were some of my favorite words! We lived on a 40-acre "fun farm," a charming almost century-old country home surrounded by a large, old-fashioned flower-bedecked yard graced with cool shade trees and a scenic pond just made for cooling off on a hot summer day. A lane meandered around a hayfield and pasture and along the surrounding woods. One of our favorite activities had always been "walking around the property" together, since we'd first moved to this dream-come-true home almost nine years before.

As we meandered slowly down the lane, chatting about insignificant matters, I sensed something significant on by husband's mind. I began to feel a tension mounting as we approached the end of our walk, an indefinable foreboding, a tautness in my husband's voice that belied the apparently trivial conversation. With studied casualness he said, "Well, I know you always want me to tell you how I feel about things, so I just wanted to tell you I don't think I love you anymore."

I can't remember what I said, but I vividly remember the sensations I experienced: the sun had fallen out of my sky, someone had kicked me in the stomach, and the immediate thought, "Oh, God, no! Here we go again!"

And so began again, for the third time in nine years, a pain-filled, drawn-out nightmare of criticisms, rejection, hurtful acts, moodiness, and ambivalence, accompanied by my bewilderment, anger, rage, disbelief, intense pain, and despair.

To all outward appearances we had the "perfect" marriage, the "perfect" life. We had met at a Christian college and married when my fiancée' graduated. In the first eight years of our marriage I had finished two years of college to get my bachelors' degree, he had completed a Masters Degree, and finally a beautiful little boy was born to us. We were always faithfully involved in service in a good church, and we prospered materially. When we bought our lovely country home I felt that God had given me "every desire of my heart": I had successfully recreated Paradise! Yet within a year I would discover my husband enmeshed in adultery and thus would begin the chain of events that culminated in his desertion of myself and our son some nine years later.

Following the fateful Spring walk described above were months of frantic effort on my part to cling to my marriage. During these days my emotions were on a continuous, non-stop high speed roller-coaster, the intensity of my feelings shaking me in a way no roller coaster ride ever had. I catapulted from livid rage to terrible hurt to abject terror to bewildered confusion - and, in rare moments of grace, to calm acceptance. Awakened very early in the morning, haunted and distracted through-out the day, and tormented into sleeplessness at night by my anxious, confused, repetitively re-cycled thoughts, I began to fear for my sanity.

Underlying all this emotional turmoil was a powerful sense of outrage at the unfairness of my situation. I had done it all right: been a good Christian, gone to a Christian college, married a Christian man, been a good Christian wife and mother, served the Lord in a good church. The Lord could not possibly allow me to lose what I had worked so hard to build for myself - the "perfect life" that was my just reward. I would just have to try harder, pray harder, seek more fervently for the magic key that would unlock my husband's frozen heart. I <u>knew</u> that I could get it all to turn out right eventually.

The sun still shone every day, despite the darkness of despair in my heart, as Spring marched inexorably into summer, and my husband marched just as inexorably toward desertion. And on a glorious, sunny August day my husband of 21 years left for work and never came home to stay again. Despite my frenzied efforts to hang on to the life we'd created for ourselves, despite the fact that I knew God was "on my side," my husband abandoned my son and I and ultimately married his secretary turned mistress.

I could not believe it. I just could not believe that God would allow me to lose my comfortable, safe, satisfying "perfect" life that we, with His help, had built for ourselves. All my previous beliefs about life and God and His intentions for us were just meaningless intellectual rubbish lying, along with my broken dreams, in ruins around my feet.

Confused by a sense of betrayal by God, I questioned His goodness, His trustworthiness. He had promised that this would never happen - hadn't he? Hadn't he guaranteed that if we walked with Him He would take care of us? That we would reap what we sowed? How could I align my terrible losses with the God of Romans 8:28 who promised that "All things work together for good to those who love him"? Further, an overwhelming sense of vulnerability haunted me. If <u>this</u> could happen to me, what other devastation was likely to occur?

Thus occurred my awakening in Paradise Lost. When my marriage ended, despite all my feverish efforts to salvage it, so also died my naive belief that this world could be a safe, predictable, controllable place to live. I faced the terrifying reality that, no matter how hard we try or how "good" we are, we cannot protect ourselves from the pain brought about because sin entered the human experience, that we truly live in" Paradise Lost". I entered a season of deep depression, as I grieved the loss of my husband and the loss of the sense of purpose and meaning that not only my marriage had given me, but also that my belief in my ability to program a safe, comfortable life had given me. I lost hope.

For Personal Reflection...

1. Loss in life is any change that causes emotional pain. Losses can be concrete or abstract. Concrete losses are things you can touch and see (home, health, a family member, marriage, etc.) Abstract losses are things invisible to the eye: a dream, an essential belief, a sacred purpose (ability to trust, belief in the goodness of God, purpose in life, etc.) We are often unaware of abstract losses. Review your life experiences to discern what concrete or abstract losses you have experienced.

2. Losses can also be gradual or sudden. We cope better with gradual loss. Consider what gradual or sudden changes or losses you have experienced.

3. Our response to loss, described as grief, touches every aspect of our human experience: emotions, physical body, behavior, thinking, and Spirit. As you consider your losses think about the way you responded in all these areas.

HOPE FOUND IN PARADISE LOST: THE METAPHOR

As I struggled through the nightmare of the death of my marriage that began with my husband's terrifying words, "I don't think I love you anymore," despite the anger, confusion, and distrust I felt toward God, I looked to Him to give me answers for the tormenting questions I found myself asking. As the days, weeks, and months rolled by, God gave me bits and pieces of thoughts, insights, and awarenesses that at first seemed haphazard, but gradually began to weave together into a "panoramic" view of life incredibly transformed from my previous perspective. I call that transformed life perspective "Hope found in Paradise lost": that is what God gave me during my personal journey through intense pain and loss. That has also become the title for a metaphor he has given me which powerfully communicates this changed life view. HopeFound is the name of my counseling practice (and, of course, Hope Found in Paradise Lost is the title of this book).

After my husband's devastating announcement that spring day, within a few months he was gone. The next several years were a roller coaster experience of hope then despair, confusion then a sense of clarity and purpose, love then hate, rage then peace. My marriage went from separation to infidelity, to cruel mistreatment of my son and myself, to divorce papers filed, ultimately to divorce, and then to the gruesome consequences as divorced played out in our lives.

Initially my faith was unstoppable: God would prevail in our behalf! I claimed all the promises in the Word that seemed to assure me of that. My son and I prayed faithfully and fervently for this wayward man, and sang praise and worship songs that reinforced our beliefs. I stayed in the Word and sought to walk through this dark season of my life in total obedience to God. Every circumstance that came along was viewed through the lens of this optimistic viewpoint. Our church family likewise joined with us in claiming ultimate restoration and healing for our family. But as my husband's choices led him farther and farther away from us, my ability to continue to cling to that position wavered.

And God was interjecting droplets of new thought, fragments of a new point of view, instances of intensely expanding perspective that confused me, intrigued me, and at times excited me with a sense of intense anticipation, and, yes, even hope. Could there be mysterious, here-to-fore unrecognized Truth from God that would heal the pain and make life meaningful again, even if the horror of divorce became reality in my life?   Could I ever trust God again?

God's tender, gradual provision of pieces of the answer to those questions took many forms. Often it came in moments of intense pain when I cried out for relief or I would die, when death seemed a welcome release. Sometimes it came as a comment heard on Christian radio or a thought in a message in church. Other times it was very personal, just for me. God several times spoke to me in complete sentences that only I could hear, at my moments of most intense need. And as the shuttle of his working in my life continued its weaving ways, a wonderful new scene formed before my desperate eyes, and made its way into my thirsting heart: hope found in Paradise lost.

THE METAPHOR

It is a beautiful Spring day, and I am very happy and secure, for I stand surrounded by a wall of protection which I have worked very hard, with God's help, to create here in Paradise Lost. I had learned very young that this place where I was born and raised was not Paradise, but Paradise Lost. I knew I needed to protect myself.

As a child in church, I had been taught the story of Adam and Eve being placed in Eden, a garden Paradise. Eden must have been an awesome place. In this Paradise-like place Adam and Eve had all their needs met perfectly. Their need for unconditional love and acceptance was met perfectly between each other and in their relationship with God. They lived in a perfectly safe environment, and had perfect emotional security in their relationships with each other and with God. They walked with God daily and carried out His directives in their daily life: incredible significance! These three core needs which we all have, from which all other needs flow-unconditional love and acceptance, security, and significance-were all perfectly met in Eden.

But when Adam and Eve chose to "do it their way" and sin entered the human race, they were booted out of Eden, the flaming swords appeared before the entrance, and never again did they set foot in the garden Paradise. They spent the rest of their existence on this planet in Paradise Lost, a place of physical discomfort and suffering, of broken relationships, of disease, of failure, of difficult, discouraging labor, of distance from God.

How they must have yearned to go back to their garden Paradise! I see them standing outside the entrance looking inside, wishing somehow to be given a second chance. As time went on, I believe they developed a focus on <u>circumstances</u> to relieve their suffering and make them comfortable: if only they could get back to Eden, they would be happy again. What they didn't realize was that the happiness and joy of Eden was not primarily in the circumstances there, but in the intimate communion they experienced with their God there.

How do I know they were like that? Because I am just like that, and all we human beings are their children, of course. Being aware of Paradise Lost, I have developed a focus on creating the perfect set of circumstances in my life to protect me from the pain of unmet needs. Even as a sincere Christian, that perspective colors my view of life. Life is about avoidance of discomfort or pain at all costs. And so I have built a wall of protection. The wall is composed of "planks", each one a part of my life which contributes to my sense of safety. These planks include self-protective behavior patterns and everything in my life which I have labored to achieve through my self-protective efforts: my Christian marriage (the most significant plank); my personal walk with God; my service in the church and elsewhere; our Christian family practices; my and my husband's degrees and careers; our financial comfort; my good health practices; my perfect parenting, my perfectionism, etc. God's role in my life is to surround my life with His love and protection. In the metaphor I see Him with His loving arms wrapped securely around my wall of protection, holding it in place.

As I stand so secure and happy in my wall of protection, the day comes when my husband says to me, "I don't think I love you anymore". And as my marriage falls to pieces I see my wall of protection fall in shambles around my feet.

I stand in the shattered ruins of my wall of protection, feeling confused, angry, utterly helpless, vulnerable, and terrified. I look toward heaven and God in absolute disbelief. How could I have worked so hard, been so obedient to God, done everything He showed me to do His way, to end up in such pain? If this could happen to me after living my life so totally in dedication to God and His will, how can I ever be safe on this planet? How absolutely meaningless and terrifyingly unsafe is this life! I have lost hope.

And God comes to me in this season of loss, pain, confusion, and fear, holds out His hand to me, and tenderly speaks. "LuAnn, I'm so glad you've finally realized that there is no such thing as a wall of protection. After all, this is Paradise Lost. That wall was just a delusion. But if you'll let go of the delusion of building walls of protection and come with me, I'll take you someplace you've never been, where you'll never be afraid again."

Indecision! Confusion! Can't I just find a new man and a new Christian marriage, and start over again building walls of protection? But the absurdity of that thought is immediately apparent to me. If it didn't work the first time, what guarantee is there it would it work a second time? I'm in crisis! I don't know which way to turn. I try to peer into the future, and see only a terrifying haze of sinister threat, as God waits so patiently for my decision.

Gradually, the haze clears, and I realize I have really only one choice. I hold out my hand so tentatively to God. I don't know if I can trust Him; I don't understand Him; but I choose to follow where He wants to lead me. Holding me by the hand, God leads me to a place right here in Paradise Lost, but deeper with Him than I have ever been before. It is a place so separated from its surroundings that it requires crossing a bridge over a river to get there. As I cross that bridge, holding God's hand, I look back at the remnants of my wall on the other side. And with a flash of insight I realize that it was never really a wall of protection-it was a prison! It had owned every day of my life. It consumed all my time and energy. I could never get free. Suddenly I feel an inexplicable sense of peace. I don't know where I'm going, but I know I'm done with the exhausting task of building walls of protection for myself. God has promised that I will never be afraid again. He will be my wall of protection. I've been set free, and it feels really good.

When I step onto the place God has led me to, the first awareness I have is that God is all I can see - he is all there is! My entire view is filled by this immense, awesome, sovereign God of the entire universe. How incredibly different from my perception of the God whose trivial task is to maintain my self-absorbed wall of protection for me! I am shamed by recognizing the naive, self-focused mold into which I had cast God.

As I adjust to this very different perception of Him, I gradually become more aware of other things in my surroundings. I see that life is a stage, and that I have a key role in a drama that God, the Supreme Director, wants to play out through my life and the lives of others on the stage. As He provides His personal, tender mentoring direction to me, I am free to yield to His guidance and influence, or to resist and "do it my way" in playing out the drama of my life. The intimacy of this personal, working relationship between myself and the sovereign God of the universe astounds me. I am overwhelmed with humble appreciation and celebration.

Eventually I begin to scan the stage that I have come to understand is my life to discover what else may be here. I notice that there are vague, indistinct shapes scattered about on the stage, obviously of no special importance, like props in the background of a play. As I observe these props more closely I make an astonishing discovery: these props are the planks that made up my delusional wall of protection! These life circumstances, accomplishments, pursuits were never meant to be a wall of protection, but just props that God wants to use as backdrop for the drama that He desires to play out on the stage of my life! This is a life-changing revelation for me. I will never be the same again.

As I take up residence in this peaceful, purposeful place I now call HopeFound, God, the Supreme Director, begins to orchestrate a three-act drama on the stage of my life. As He mentors me in my development as a participant in His drama, and oversees the circumstances that are the props that appear on the stage of my life, He seeks my cooperation with Him to accomplish His eternal sovereign purposes, beginning with Act One: "Knowing God".

I do know Him as God and Savior, and that is the starting point. But God wants me to know Him as this immense, sovereign God who is the absolute authority of my life, no holds barred. He wants me to trust who He is and believe absolutely in His sovereign capability to accomplish spiritual, eternal good, whatever the circumstances on the stage of my life. As I come to agree with Him that His spiritual, eternal purposes are the greatest good that my life can experience, even greater than any plank from my delusional wall of protection, I thus yield willingly and expectantly to His control over every nuance of my life. The drama in Act One, played out by the Supreme Director and me, leads to that denouement of brokenness and yielding, transforming me into a serene, trusting, yielded heart.

A yielded heart is a pliable heart, and thus I am now prepared to experience Act Two: "Being changed by him". As I truly know God as the supreme, sovereign ruler of the entire universe and of my life, and continue to yield to Him, through His spirit He is able to gradually transform my self-absorbed, mundane being into a child of God who is increasingly more like the Father everyday. He is able to recreate Himself in me, imperfectly, it is true, but far more like Him than I've ever been before. The drama in Act Two, played out on the stage of my life by the Supreme Director and me, climaxes with the metamorphosis of a beautiful spirit increasingly like Him.

As surely as dark turns to dawn, Act Three inevitably follows: "Being used by Him". I have come to truly know

Him as my personal, sovereign, universe-ruling God; I have been transformed by that sweet relationship with Him into his image; it is now inevitable that I will be a powerful tool in His hand to accomplish His purposes in the family, friends, community and corner of the world that He allows on the stage of my life in HopeFound. The climactic Act Three is the pinnacle toward which the whole drama has been progressing. As surely as Christ's season of life on this planet led triumphantly to death on a cross and resurrection to new life, so our season of life in HopeFound is meant to lead triumphantly to this death to self, and resurrection to His life.

The most startling reality in HopeFound is that pursuit of "Paradise recreated" becomes increasingly insignificant, compared to the awesomeness of experiencing God changing me and using me to accomplish incredible things of eternal significance. All the comforts that we rightly yearn for-good health, good marriages, financial security, well-behaved kids, career success, etc.-must be willingly released into God's provident hands, trusting that if He chooses to remove these "props" or allows them to be removed, He does so knowing that only through this loss can He accomplish the Spiritual good He knows is best.

The awareness and acceptance that God's primary goal in HopeFound, here in Paradise Lost, is not the fairytale ending, "and they all lived happily ever after", but spiritual, eternal good, is a life-changing serendipitous experience that transforms my attitude toward discomfort, pain and human suffering. Before, pain was an enemy, to be avoided at all cost. Pain caused questions about the goodness of God. Here in HopeFound, pain is embraced and celebrated as the conduit of God's best for me, a gift that in His wisdom He knows I could receive no other way. For the first time, James 1:2-4 makes perfectly good sense: "Count it all joy when you fall into various trials and testings, because you know that the testing of your faith develops perseverance,

and perseverance must complete it work so tha
perfect and mature, not lacking anything."

The day comes in HopeFound when the c
down on the drama of my life, and I leave this sau planet
and enter eternal life in the presence of my heavenly Father.
For the first time in my existence, I experience perfect,
immeasurable joy - comfort and pleasure beyond my wildest
imagination! My loving heavenly Father has always cared
intensely about my "comfort" - even in the midst of my pain
He has been preparing this incredible place for me to experience fulfillment "to the max" for all eternity! In this place
of indescribable pleasure I discover that every nuance of
my yielding and cooperation with God, to accomplish His
purposes in Paradise Lost, has accompanied me into this
place, and shapes the pleasure of my eternal experience! Paul
said in Romans 8:18: "I consider that our present sufferings
are not worth comparing with the glory that will be revealed
in us." As I look back at my life experiences in Paradise
Lost, all the discomfort, hurt, and suffering seem so incredibly insignificant in light of this awesome, eternal heaven in
which I now dwell with God.

For Personal Reflection...

1. Listed below are key concepts from the
   "HopeFound in Paradise Lost" metaphor. Assess
   with genuine honesty where you stand today in
   terms of believing and/or experiencing each of
   the concepts noted.

   ⅄ The pursuit of "Paradise Recreated" is a prison
   of self-centeredness that wants to own us.

⋏ The disappointments and hurts of life can eventually so discourage us that we give up being able to recreate paradise.

⋏ This "letting go" sets us free from the prison of self-serving life pursuits to focus above all else on God's purposes for our lives.

⋏ God's purposes for us are threefold:
1. Knowing Him and yielding to Him
2. Being changed by Him
3. Being used by Him

⋏ Eternity will be pleasurable beyond imagination and will convert all our cooperation with God into eternal reward.

BIBLICAL FOUNDATION FOR THE METAPHOR

though my discovery of the truths found in the "Hope Found in Paradise Lost" metaphor was like a revelation to me, in reality I had read the very scriptures that proclaim these truths over and over, and even memorized several of them, yet never saw the "panoramic view" that God wove for me in my season of loss. For the record I want to reference several passages supporting the metaphor.

In the discourse between God and Job in Job 38-42 God powerfully declares His sovereignty over the entire universe and right to rule in the affairs of men because of who He is, and in contrast how markedly insignificant we are, resulting in Job's humble response,

"I know that you can do all things; no plan of yours can be thwarted. You asked, 'Who is this that obscures my counsel without knowledge?' Surely I spoke of things I did not understand, things too wonderful for me to know. You said, 'Listen now, and I will speak; I will question you, and you shall answer me.' My ears had heard of you, but now my eyes have seen you. Therefore I despise myself and repent in dust and ashes."

Job, a very righteous man before his terrible sufferings, after he lost everything experienced a serendipitous moment:

he saw God as He really is, the absolute sovereign Ruler of the entire universe and of his life. Dealing with his grief transformed his view of God. He experienced the metaphor's Act One: "Knowing God." To this God there is only one appropriate response - unquestioning yielding.

Matthew 22 describes a number of exchanges between Jesus and the Sadducees, the cynics of His time. They asked Jesus the question, "Which is the greatest commandment in the Law?" Unwittingly they created the opportunity for Jesus to document for them and for all time His highest intention for His followers. Jesus resounding response, "Love the Lord with all your heart and with all your soul and with all your mind" forever defined this highest calling of life, the pursuit of an intensely personal relationship with our God. Act One: "Knowing Him" depicts this highest life goal.

The verse I claimed as my "life verse" was Galatians 5:22, 23: "But the fruit of the Spirit is love, joy, peace, patience, kindness, goodness, faithfulness, gentleness, and self-control." The power of God through His Spirit to transform my self-centered, sinful personality to His very nature is proclaimed here, as symbolized in Act Two: "Being Changed By Him". Additional Scripture that proclaims this truth is found in 1 Peter 1:6,7: "...you may have had to suffer grief in all kinds of trials. These have come so that your faith-of greater worth than gold, which perishes even though refined by fire-may be proved genuine...". God's working in the painful circumstances of our lives to bring about positive spiritual change is declared here, as well as in the classic verse, Romans 8:28, 29: "And we know that in all things God works for the good of those who love Him, who have been called according to His purpose. For those God fore-knew he also predestined to be conformed to the likeness of His Son...".

The verse previously referenced, James 1:2-4: "Consider it pure joy, my brothers, whenever you face trials of many kinds, because you know that the testing of your faith develops perseverance. Perseverance must finish its work so that you may be mature and complete, not lacking anything", makes the remarkable statement that we must accept the painful tests of life and view them as cause to rejoice because we know that God is changing us spiritually through our suffering. Act Two again! Romans 5:3,4 which says, "Not only so, but we also rejoice in our sufferings, because we know that suffering produces perseverance; perseverance, character; and character, hope," also affirms the same theme. Many other Scriptures could be noted throughout the Word repeatedly emphasizing this essential life truth for those of us who believe.

Joseph, the favored son of Abraham, was sold into slavery by his jealous brethren; taken to Egypt and purchased by Potiphar, a high official; falsely accused by Potiphar's wife and imprisoned; ultimately released; eventually became the second-in-command in Egypt; and finally was able to save his family from starvation because of his position. Joseph lost his home, his family, his reputation, years of his life spent in prison. Yet in Genesis 50:20 he says to his brethren, "You intended to harm me, but God intended it for good, to accomplish what is now being done..." Joseph in this insightful comment defines for us the truth of Act Three: "Being Used by Him". Through all these tragic circumstances in his life he came to accept that they were unimportant compared to what God was able to do through them: prepare him for service, and place him exactly where He needed him to be to accomplish the awesome task of saving the chosen people of God, his family.

In a story with a very similar ending, Esther, a Jewess, becomes the favored queen of Persia, to soon find herself embroiled in political intrigue that threatens to destroy her people, again God's chosen people. Esther courageously defends her people and is able to rescue them from destruction. The words of Mordecai, her Jewish uncle, are used by God to challenge her to courageous action: "...And who knows but that you have come to royal position for such a time as this?"[1] With wisdom meant not only for Esther but for us, Mordecai says that the circumstances in her life which led her to the throne of Persia had been orchestrated by God to allow her "to be used by Him" to defend his people from annihilation.

Solomon spent a lifetime and all his resources on a quest to understand the meaning of life. With inspired wisdom he concluded that all the pursuits of life- riches, knowledge, pleasure, folly, toil-are meaningless, and ends Ecclesiastes with this pinnacle statement found in Ecclesiastes 12:13, " Now all has been heard; here is the conclusion of the matter: fear God and keep his commandments, for this is the whole duty of man." After spending a lifetime building incredible walls of protection, for Solomon all those life pursuits became meaningless -insignificant props on a stage, backdrop for the only thing that mattered, obeying and serving God. Being used by God was the only thing Solomon ultimately found worth living for.

In Jesus' discourse in Matthew 6 He contrasted two kingdoms, God and mammon, and concluded with Matthew 6:33, which says, "But seek first His Kingdom and His righteousness, and all these things will be given to you as well". This verse defines His highest priority for us, his followers: yielding to Him as our sovereign God and making our service to Him first in our life, above any other earthly concern. I Thessalonians 5:18, "Give thanks in all circumstances, for this is God's will for you in Christ Jesus," likewise reflects a heart yielded totally to God's greater purposes in life.

Subsequent to my divorce, I eventually finished a Masters Degree in Counseling, and have been a Licensed Professional Counselor in private practice for a number of years. The wisdom and "Hope Found in Paradise Lost" metaphor discovered through the experiences of my years of suffering continue to be regularly recycled into the lives of my clients. I claim for my clients in the midst of their suffering 2 Corinthians 1: 3,4,

"Praise be to the God and Father of our Lord Jesus Christ, the Father of compassion and the God of all comfort, who comforts us in all our troubles, so that we can comfort those in any trouble with the comfort we ourselves have received from God." God says that our life experiences of suffering are teaching us how to comfort those who suffer, with His comfort!

Joseph experienced incredible suffering in his season of preparation; Esther experienced favor and honor in her season of preparation. Solomon experienced unsurpassed wealth and wisdom; I experienced desertion and divorce. Whatever God allows on the stage of our lives, whether blessing or a curse, He intends to use it as a refining fire in His preparation of us for the eternally important tasks that lie ahead for us. God is always about the task of preparing us and then using us for service to Him! Sadly, loss of the things we hold the most dear seems to be the most potent tool God has to break our obsessive stranglehold on the things of this life, and bring our heart's focus in line with His eternal plans.

Notes
[1] Esther 4:14

For Personal Reflection:
1. Does this chapter help you clearly see the pervasive emphasis throughout Scripture on the "HopeFound perspective?"

2. What Bible character and/or Scripture teaches you this message the most powerfully?

WHY WALLS OF PROTECTION IN PARADISE LOST

The need to build walls of protection is rooted in experiences in our lives starting in infancy. Let's revisit previous comments made about Adam and Eve's experience of having their core needs perfectly met in Eden. I identified three core needs from which all other needs flow: the need for unconditional love and acceptance, the need for physical and emotional security, and the need for significance and meaning. In Eden, the garden Paradise, every variation on these three needs was perfectly met. Not so in Paradise Lost! As a matter of fact, every human need is either <u>imperfectly</u> met, or not met at all in Paradise Lost, starting with the first tender months of our earthly life. Even preborn infants begin experiencing unmet needs before birth, based on their parents' choices in such areas as nutrition, toxic chemicals, and the emotional climate they perceive while in the womb.

From the moment of conception, and then from the moment of birth, each uniquely designed human being needs certain kinds of experiences in life to flourish and grow according to God's intention for his/her life. As a new life very precisely designed by the creator-God, each of us has very precise needs at each stage of life which, if properly met, allow him to accomplish what developmental theorists call "developmental tasks." These tasks are in various categories and are sequential, building on the accomplishment of each preceding task in each stage of life, in order to move to the next developmental task as the next stage of life is experienced. To arrive at adulthood absolutely complete physically, emotionally, mentally, socially, relationally, and spiritually, all the needs of each stage of development must be perfectly met, beginning in the womb!

This, of course, absolutely never happens here in Paradise Lost. The impact of the presence of sin, falleness, and death interferes at every point. The genetic code we receive at conception is marked with the death-requirement; life in the womb includes deliberate choices and chance events which mar preparation for life beyond the womb. From the moment of birth our parents, family, and a myriad of life circumstances create a montage of elements and experiences which vary from slightly imperfect to horribly damaging in their ability to meet our basic developmental needs. This montage of life experiences cannot be a perfect environment, able to transmit to us and replicate in us the perfect love, safety, security and significance we desperately need. Thus, very early on we begin to experience "pain": the shortfall between what we need and what we receive. This pain can be consciously experienced as physical or emotional discomfort or distress, or may only be experienced unconsciously, due to repression. But whatever the case, pain, in this sense, is the force which empowers the building of great walls of protection. At a very young age we unconsciously begin to focus on self-protection, the controlling of our environment in order to prevent further pain. We've entered the business of building walls of protection.

Tom and Beverly Rodgers, in their insightful book, Soul-Healing love,[2] employ a concept which fits well with this discussion. They refer to "soul-wounds", which they define as "unmet needs in childhood which wound the soul and cause us to be over-reactive to those needs in adulthood." Let's look at some practical examples of "soul-wounding" life experiences which lead to over-reaction, or wall-building.

An infant is repeatedly left alone, hungry and crying, while parents pursue drug addiction. The soul-wound of abandonment is created, a deep mistrust that people he needs and loves will not stay in his life, causing him to cling to relationships in an obsessive way, building codependency into his wall of protection to imprison people, in order to prevent the pain of loss.

A young child is constantly insulted with demeaning names and labels, creating a deep sense of shame about who she is. This soul-wound of worthlessness and shame leads to perfectionism, an attempt to build walls of accomplishment to protect from the pain of the shame-message of worthlessness.

A young girl is repeatedly sexually molested by her grandfather each time her family visits with him. Terrified by her helpless inability to defend herself from assault, she matures into an aggressive, dominating woman who marries a very passive man, determined to use control as part of her wall of protection from the pain of abuse in any form.

Because his father doubts that he is really his biological son, a boy constantly experiences being rebuffed in his efforts to be close to his Dad. Though his father provides for him, there is no emotional bond of affection between them. This soul-wound of rejection causes him to include emotional detachment in adult relationships as part of his protective wall, shielding himself from further pain of rejection.

The vast majority of soul-wounds are inflicted in the context of important relationships in childhood, since therein lies the potential for our core human needs to be foundationally met or not met. Thus, the illustrations of soul-wounding experiences shared above involve a significant relationship's failure to meet a core need, followed by the child's relational style adapting to protect himself from experiencing that pain again. Occasionally, circumstances rather than significant relationships become the source of soul-wounding pain; some aspect of the situation prevents the child experiencing fulfillment of basic developmental needs.

Poverty can be devastating to a child's sense of acceptance, security and significance. An orphan boy goes to school with no lunch, no socks, no bath, experiencing humiliating rejection and shame. Life becomes a fanatical effort to accumulate hordes of money to protect from repetition of that hellish scene. His wall of protection is rich with material comforts and investments.

A boy's school experiences of lack of progress and failure lead to intense feelings of incompetence and inadequacy, causing him to retreat into alcohol and other addictions as an adult, using the plank of addiction in his wall of protection to hide from any threat of pain caused by further life experiences of failure or incompetence.

An unexpected relocation to a new town at a critical time in a child's life; a siblings' chronic serious illness or rebellion; significant societal events such as war, disaster; mental illness in the extended family; a parent's chronic infidelity or serious illness-these are some of many examples of circumstances which, though not directed toward a child, nevertheless have the capacity to impact her life in soul-wounding ways.

The planks we incorporate in our walls of protection are determined by the nature of our soul-wounding childhood experiences. As in the previous illustrations, whatever the unmet need of childhood, the methods of protection we build into our lives will reflect our need to shield ourselves from that specific type of pain. These hiding strategies we choose to protect ourselves from further pain in life are not standardized but individualized; nevertheless, there is a pattern to that choice. In responding to any particular unmet need, a child will typically skew to an extreme on a continuum, from intensely needing and seeking after that need to be met, to disavowing that need altogether. The ability to stay balanced gets lost in the pain. In all the above illustrations of childhood soul-wounding circumstances, I described one direction of adaptation the child may take. It is just as likely that he/she may adapt in the opposite direction. An abandoned child may either cling to relationships or withdraw from needing them; a sexually abused girl may either seek control as a protection from further pain, or become completely boundaryless in relationships because of her inability to defend healthy boundaries in childhood. Significantly soul-wounding childhood experiences always shift our patterns of behavior to extremes on a continuum.

This out-of-balance skewing results in several other general patterns of "plank-formation" in walls of protection. Some wounded travelers in Paradise Lost become very relationally needy, manipulating people in enmeshing ways, seeking protection through sometimes smothering intimacy. Others move away from people into pursuit of careers, accomplishments, pleasure, etc.; they choose to not need people, as protection from further relationship-inflicted pain. A number of other similar contrasting dyads could be noted, such as passivity versus aggression; intellectualization versus emotionality; ambition versus aimlessness.

Thus, the planks that make up our walls of protection in Paradise Lost are a very complex, little-understood amalgamation of personality traits, relational styles, and life activities, pursuits, and goals. Unconsciously driving all of this human activity and behavior is the cry of the wounded heart for protection, for succor, for healing.

When talking to clients about this sad human dynamic I describe it as "Satan's clever scheme." God created us to know Him, and through relationship with Him to find perfect fulfillment of all our needs. Satan takes the pain of unmet needs brought about by sin's presence in human experience and uses it to stir up intense self-protective patterns of response in us. These self-protective behaviors becomes the driving force of our lives, more powerful than God's voice wooing us to pursue His purposes for us. And so each of us, damaged by the impact of sin's presence in our human experience, likewise become people whose sinful self-interest inflicts soul-wounding pain on those whose lives we touch, and the disease keeps getting passed on and on and on…and God's greater purposes for our lives get relegated to the "also-ran" category. How very clever Satan is!

Notes
[2] Rodgers, Beverly and Tom, <u>Soul-Healing Love</u>. San Jose Resource Publications, Inc. 1998

For Personal Reflection…

1. "Why Walls of Protection in Paradise Lost?" identified 3 core needs - unconditional love, security, and significance:

    * How was your need for <u>unconditional</u> love met/not met in childhood?

        By your mother? by your father? by siblings? by others?

    * How was your need for security met?
        Were you physically safe?
        Were you properly cared for (fed, clothed, etc)?
        Were you emotionally safe?

    * How was your need for significance met in childhood?
        Were you treated with respect?
        Were you given adequate time and attention?
        Were you listened to?
        Were you given responsibilities?

Did you have successes and if so were your successes recognized? Were you/your thoughts/your feelings affirmed?

2. Think about your childhood from earliest days and remember any circumstances in your or your family's life that caused you "pain", as described in the chapter.

   * something significant that you really wanted and weren't able to have.
   * something stressful you really wanted to change and couldn't.

3. How did you cope or adapt to these unmet needs then?

   * Do you recognize any resultant "out-of-balance skewing" in your personality, character, lifestyle or relational style, e.g. relationally needy vs. detached, etc.?
   * Did they cause formation of "planks" in a "wall of protection"?

WHEN THE WALL
FALLS DOWN

In the metaphor, when my husband abandons me, my wall of protection falls in shambles around my feet, symbolizing the loss of the delusion that life is predictable, manageable, under control. Until that time in my life, I truly believed that all my wall-building efforts would successfully insulate me from the pain running rampant in Paradise Lost. But when the pain of desertion and divorce found its way past, through, or over my wall of protection, I could not delude myself any longer that I had magical power to orchestrate all the happy life outcomes that I wanted. I was engulfed with terror, despair, and hopelessness.

The circumstances that crumble great but delusional walls of protection vary in each person's life. A diagnosis of a life-threatening disease for myself or someone I love; a financial loss that threatens my financial survival; being passed over at work for the promotion I had worked so hard for and knew I deserved; my child's exhausting, discouraging rebellion; my parent's failing health; unsettling societal crises, such as September 11,2001; these and numberless other scenarios have the power to stir in us a dreadful awareness that we are not as omnipotent as we have blithely assumed that we are.

A combination of genetics, personal history, and coincidence prescribes at what point a difficult circumstance will be the "last straw" that eliminates the delusion that I can control the pain-factor in life. Some people continue to believe in magical walls of protection despite numerous crises; others become dis-believers after only one relatively minor crisis or loss. Some die still fighting against the truth of their own vulnerability. Yet waking up to that truth is the best thing that can happen to us.

I read a number of years ago that the Chinese language uses two symbols to write the word "crisis". One is the symbol for the word danger, the other the symbol for the word opportunity. How true! In a crisis, there is the danger that the coping strategies I use will destroy myself or others. There is also the wonderful opportunity to cope through life-altering changes that make me stronger, better, more Godly, etc. A major life crisis is a wonderful opportunity to shed my life-consuming focus on my delusional ability to program the "good life", and recognize for the first time how fruitless and truly meaningless that pursuit really is.

Facing the truth that I am not in control of my life and cannot be is perhaps the most significant crisis in life. It is an existential crisis rather than just a circumstantial one that almost always leads to deep depression. Depression is seen by many therapists as a result of pervasive, inescapable powerlessness As a therapist many of my clients come in complaining of depression resulting from a life situation in which they experienced that kind of powerlessness. A wife who has "stood by her man" through several years of cancer treatment loses him to the disease; a man loses his third job in ten years; an alcoholic goes "off the wagon" after several years of sobriety; a marriage of many years ends because a partner is unfaithful. Often, underlying these circumstances that caused intense emotional pain and exhaustion is a meaning being attached to that loss which accounts for the terribly deep level of depression: "I have almost no control over what life does to me". I believe this type of depression is what has been called "the dark season of the soul". It is a "good" depression because it allows that soul to ultimately be freed from bondage to circumstances to pursue the greater more noble purposes for which it was created by God.

After my husband left me, I awoke every day for months from tormented sleep to the agonizing thought, "I wish I were dead". I was in my "dark season of the soul". When I emerged from that dark tunnel I had finally shed my obsession with pursuing my comfort-driven plans as life's highest calling. I'd been set free to pursue with abandon God's highest calling to relinquish my life into His sovereign, eternal purposes. The crisis had passed. I was not afraid anymore. I've never been afraid since.

For Personal Reflection...

1. "When the Wall Falls Down" describes circumstances in life that can lead us into "the dark season of the soul".

   ⋏ Have you had that experience? In what circumstance/s?

   ⋏ How did it affect you?

2. Have you experienced a crisis that involved both danger and opportunity?

   ⋏ How did you respond? How did it turn out?

3. Have you given up the delusion that you have the power to program the comfortable, pleasant life

circumstances that you desire, that life is about building walls of protection?

ACT ONE:
KNOWING HIM

In the HopeFound metaphor, the first act of the enfolding drama that signifies my life is "Knowing Him". The foundational, life-changing knowledge God wants us to get deeply rooted into our hearts is to know Him as He truly is. He uses His personal involvement with us and the props that represent our life circumstances to teach us about Himself. Only as we come to truly know Him can He continue to implement the "perfect" script for our lives written in eternity past.

Many of those who come to a saving knowledge of God through faith in Jesus Christ never get beyond a superficial, inaccurate understanding of His true nature. Unfortunately, in so many ways life spawns deceptive, inaccurate, and damaging aspects of our image of God.

Even within the Christian church, teaching and experience can contribute to false perceptions of the nature of God. Some churches foster images of Him as punishing, angry, vindictive; or loving, permissive, enabling. "Prosperity preaching" can create the delusion that God guarantees that our faith can ensure continued material prosperity. Rigid adherence to a church-prescribed list of do's and don'ts is presented as the means to pleasing God by some sects. Others teach that total separation from the conveniences of modern society is what God demands as obedience to Him. Faith-healers guarantee that with your and their faith God can be programmed to heal our diseases. Experiences within the life of the church can promulgate erroneous beliefs about God, based on observation of God's supposed servants. Does their character reflect His character?

Our experiences with our earthly fathers can unconsciously create an image of God's nature based on the way they fulfilled their role as father in our lives. Critical, impossible-to-please fathers breed submerged perceptions in their children's' souls of a Father-God just like their earthly father. Life experiences for these misled offspring are then unknowingly imprinted with this image of a God who carries the ghost of their fathers' rejection. Likewise, absent, indifferent fathers who abandon us literally and/or emotionally create a God in their children's' hearts who cannot be trusted to be there and care. He is a distant, impersonal, unable-to-be-known deity. When a kind-hearted but ineffectual father can easily be manipulated and overruled, his children may see God as impotent, and disregard Him.

Earthly fathers who verbally, physically, or sexually abuse their children often kill hope in these children's' souls. God, the only force powerful enough to combat the evil, the supposed source of good, and their only hope, is also a Father, and therein lies a paradox which they will not be able to unravel. Experiences with their fathers will unconsciously permeate the image of this all-powerful God with the desire and capacity to hurt, which irreparably kills hope for a God who loves and thus will rescue them from pain. Instead He becomes another potential source of pain from whom they need to hide. Atheism can be a necessary dogma to "kill" a God who would hurt them if they allowed Him to exist. How many of the proponents of the "God is Dead" movement had fathers who abused them?

Messages received from the society in which we live can also color our image of God. Modern-day America is replete with a confusing melee of messages about the existence and character of God. Certainly the most highly-promulgated position is that God is a relatively minor to non-existent player in the life of society, and needs to be kept out of the public arena. Recent judicial decisions such as taking God out of our Pledge of Allegiance and removing the Ten Commandments from government buildings reflect that position. Additionally, the entertainment industry's representations of those who proclaim belief in God are consistently ridiculing and belittling. Belief in God is often treated as ignorant and even downright dangerous. Adherence to Biblical standards of morality and practice is overtly mocked and indirectly subverted. The news media typically twist their presentation of the news to reflect negatively on issues of moral or spiritual significance and on those courageous individuals who stand up in defense of them. The academic, scientific, and intellectual communities likewise make their contribution to the confusion about God with their assertions based on human reasoning and theory rather than absolute truth. The theory of evolution, as an example, changes God from a personal, relational Father-God to an impersonal force that set creation in motion, but did not father a unique race created in His own image.

True, Christians of conviction are a force to be reckoned with in both political and public life, striving to be "salt and light" to a culture beset with rampant materialism, sexual obsession, and self-absorption. Yet despite the efforts of many Godly leaders both political and religious, it's nearly impossible to see the truth about the sovereign God of the universe by looking through the lens of public life in America today.

The ugliness of sin in its most dreadful forms causes many people to question the goodness and even existence of God. Rape, murder, abuse, and other heinous crimes assault and horrify the soul, causing even those who only see it on the news

47

to shudder and wonder "Where is God? How could He allow such wickedness to go unchecked?" Holding Him responsible, if He exists at all, for all the evil in the world, these disillusioned pilgrims in Paradise Lost resign themselves to no remedy for the darkness of the world in which they live. God is either impotent, indifferent, or nonexistent.

Unanswered prayers for relief from tormenting life circumstances, for things to get better, can likewise deaden the heart's ability to trust in a God who seems to be absent or not listening.

Comments which imply reprehensible aspects of God's nature can be made in ignorance yet have a devastating effect on a person's concept of God. Parents have often said to children after a death, "God loved her/him so much He wanted her to come and be with Him in heaven." What does this say about a God so selfish He inflicts all this suffering so He can have what He wants? "You won't go to heaven if you don't stop doing that" is a very misleading comment which implies a God who is conditional in His love and vindictive as well. Many other illustrations could be shared of well-meaning attempts by parents to communicate about the existence of God, which can foster an image of Him that causes their children to fear and even reject Him.

In the midst of all this confusion about Him, God wants to be known accurately and intimately. He uses His Word, His Spirit, His people, His church, our life circumstances, His intervention in our lives, and our response to Him, to write on our receptive hearts the eternal story of Himself, as He seeks to draw us into a deeply personal relationship with Him.

God did that with me in my journey to HopeFound. Like so many who have grown up in a Christian church, I had learned Bible stories but never really comprehended the full, sweeping story the Bible tells. I had received bits and pieces of truth but the integration of those pieces was vague and incomplete.

The Bible does tells an integrated story, beginning in Genesis 1 and ending in Revelation 22. Revealed in that remarkable story is the essence of who God truly is. Following is that story.

"In the beginning God created heaven and earth."[3] God has always existed since eternity past. He existed as a trinity of Himself, the Word who later became the God-man Christ Jesus, and the Holy Spirit. They are indivisible and one in essence. They are pure holy love. In God's divine language holiness and love are almost synonymous. Holiness is pure good. God's kind of love is defined best by the Greek word *agape* in the New Testament. It is not an emotion but is the choice to do pure good-what is ultimately spiritually best-for those whom you love, even at sacrifice to oneself. Holiness is a character trait within, love is the acting out of that trait. Love requires a recipient.

At a point of time in eternity past this Godhead chose to create a universe and populate it with humankind. They worked powerfully and harmoniously together in this awesome, colossal, creative endeavor. And they were very pleased with their work. They saw it all as good.[4]

However, they were not blind to the trouble that lay ahead for this human race. Because Satan and his followers had vacated Heaven and were present and at work in the universe,[5] it was inevitable that the riptide of sin invading the human race would occur. God had created these remarkable creatures in His image with a dual purpose in mind - that He have fellowship with them, and that through that fellowship the beauty of His holiness be increased throughout His universe. Satan intended to attempt to thwart God's plan to magnify His beautiful holiness through this race He had created. God knew that the human heart would become the battleground between His holiness and Satan's evil. He knew that this beloved race, whose parents Adam and Eve He had placed in a perfect garden, were no match for the power of evil they would be facing. Because though marvelous in design and stamped with His image, they had one fatal flaw. They were not perfect and therefore capable of sinlessness. God knew that Satan's temptation to respond arrogantly, selfishly rather than holy would be successful, and would begin a never-ending ripple effect of sin begetting sin begetting sin throughout human history. The one thing God could not do was make them perfect. Only God is perfect. And being perfectly holy, God hates sin with an awesome passion. Its presence in these humans' lives would destroy any possibility of relationship.

What an incredible conversation must have ensued as the Godhead considered this dilemma! How could they enable this flawed human race to have righteousness that would overcome the power of sin? How could they protect God's intention to know and fellowship with mankind and thus expand the presence of holiness throughout the universe for all eternity?

Right from the beginning they had a plan.[6] It was a terrible plan, full of violent, intense pain for all of them, because it involved separation and death. Yet they were unanimous in agreeing that it was the only way. The Word, who had been one with the Father and the Spirit for all time, would come to this planet at an appointed time, would take on flesh and live a sinless life as both God and man, and would die a criminal's death that killed divinity. Jesus Christ would hang on a cross and absorb the killing hatred and wrath of the Father for the sin of all mankind. God would turn His back on Himself and experience the incomprehensibly painful schizophrenia of hatred and rejection within the Godhead for the first time in all eternity . They agreed that this divine death would be acceptable as a substitutionary payment for the deserved eternal separation from God and His holiness that sin's corruption in human lives would require.

What an incredible decision! What incomprehensible love! Not the wimpy, spineless "love" that self-absorbed mankind usually practices, that only loves when it gets what it wants. Not the coddling love that's only desire is to make the other feel good. This supreme act of sacrificial giving would define for all eternity the true essence of love, *agape* love: unconditionally doing what's spiritually best for the other, no matter what the personal cost. We humans can never understand the suffering that the Godhead experienced in this monumental sacrifice. We get a glimmer of how profound Jesus knew the pain would be when, in the Garden of Gethsemane just before His betrayal and arrest, he begged God, if it were possible, to let this cup pass from Him. But he had known for all eternity that this moment in time would come, and He was willing to go through it. "Nevertheless, not My will but Thine."[7]

In preparation for this magnificent act of sacrificial love the Godhead guided this beloved race of mankind through many experiences, all intended to point toward His future salvation. A chosen race was delegated to be the human ancestry of the Messiah, the Savior. God instituted the law and the system of sacrifices as an incredible metaphor to point toward the coming "lamb that would take away the sins of the world."[8] He demonstrated to His chosen people time and again, as recorded through-out the Old Testament, that they were unable to achieve righteousness on their own and needed the promised Savior whose coming was prophesied throughout human history.

"When the fullness of time was come,"[9] the fulfillment of all God's promises began at a manger in Bethlehem with angels singing in ecstatic joy, led Jesus to a cross on Golgotha where the horrible deed was done, to the pit of hell, and ultimately to an empty tomb and resurrection to eternal life. Jesus' victory over the "sting of death" purchased eternal spiritual life for all who would believe. A transaction planned and facilitated by all the powers of Heaven and fought to the death by all the powers of hell. But God was victorious. The dilemma had been resolved. Relationship could be restored.

God's awesome beautiful holiness could be recreated in His beloved human race and spread throughout His universe. God was very, very happy.

God used the disciples and other called apostles to establish the Church, the medium through which the gospel, "the good news", of His salvation would be told to all humankind around the world. To ensure the preservation of Truth for future generations He inspired writers during early church history to write what became the New Testament. In it He documented the life, death, and resurrection of Jesus Christ, the establishment of the Church and the doctrine which formed its foundation, and the prophetic story of the remaining chapters of human history yet to be fulfilled.

Embedded in that writing was the description of how God's most treasured purposes could be achieved: the forming of a fellowship of believers and the transmission of His holiness to them and through them. Through "saving faith" in who Jesus Christ is and in His substitutionary death and resurrection, resulting in the indwelling Holy Spirit taking up residence in their hearts, believers could be transformed increasingly into the image of God Himself! Both individually and collectively, as the Church, these believers would revolutionize the world with this God-given holiness.

This passion for the reproduction of holiness drives the heart of God for all eternity. It is His consuming fire. It will be achieved perfectly in heaven - Paradise recreated - and become the basis for eternal sweet communion between redeemed man and his Maker. Thus God must invest every capacity He has, use every circumstance man experiences, to facilitate this spiritual transformation here in Paradise Lost. Eternal glory and joy depend on it. His grief over the necessary suffering along the way cannot be allowed to be a deterrent. Love allows Him to do no less. Love prevails.

In HopeFound God's foundational desire for us is that we know Him as He truly is. His prodigious, magnificent creation reveals Him. Jesus Christ, God in the flesh, reveals Him. The written Word reveals Him. His working in our lives for our spiritual, eternal good reveals Him. God is the powerful, pulsating core of pure, holy love that exists at the center of the universe. That holy goodness emanates from His being throughout creation like light piercing the darkness. He does not come into our lives uninvited, unwelcome, or rejected, but when He is sought everyone He touches, everyone that reaches his hand to touch Him, is penetrated with that love. God is love.

In every moment of every life God continually works to be truly known. Whatever step each of us is on in our personal journey to fully knowing him, God uses every means available to him to woo us to take the next step.

Some of you reading this book have never taken the step from spiritual death to spiritual life. While you may have been on a journey toward God, you have never responded to the Spirit's gentle voice saying, "This is truth-believe it, receive it." Beginning our eternal relationship with God involves being born spiritually. Jesus said "Ye must be born again. That which is born of the flesh is flesh, that which is born of the spirit is spirit."[10] We have physical life when we are born physically, but we need a spiritual birth into eternal life. Paul tells us in Ephesians that we are spiritually dead in our sins until by his grace God makes us alive in Christ.[11] The transforming element that births us into God's eternal family is faith. "Without faith it is impossible to please God[12]...faith cometh by hearing...the Word of God."[13]Just as physical birth occurs at a specific moment in time after months of preparation, spiritual birth occurs at a specific moment in time after a season of preparation leading to faith being created in our soul. Faith is the conviction that what the Bible says about God, Jesus Christ and the Holy Spirit is truth, and that I need and do choose to receive the gift of salvation made possible by Jesus' death, burial and resurrection, and to turn my life over to God as his obedient servant forever. Our "saving faith" invites the Holy Spirit of God to take up residence in our previously dead soul and we become a living spirit and a member of God's family for eternity. This life-giving transaction that places us in God's eternal family is described in John 1:12, "Yet to all who received Him, to those who believed in his name, he gave the right to become children of God."

This moment of spiritual birth can be consummated through a simple prayer such as, "Heavenly Father, I believe that you exist as the supreme creator and ruler of the universe, and that you created me and want me in your spiritual family. I believe that my sinful nature stands in the way of that eternal relationship, and that Jesus' death, burial and resurrection was for me, to resolve the sin-problem between you and me. At this moment I ask you to forgive me my sins and receive me into your family. I now give myself to you as your obedient servant for life. Thank you for the awesome gift of eternal life with you. Amen".

Speaking a prayer such as this to God is the moment of spiritual birth. For some people that moment is accompanied by intense joyous emotion. For others there is just the quiet conviction that a life-changing spiritual transaction with God has occurred. It is important to note that it is not emotion that saves us. It is faith.

God pursues us. The next passage in our spiritual journey may be saving faith through believing what the Bible says about Jesus Christ and the Godhead, or the progressive steps of closer and closer understanding of, communion with, and obedience to God. Whatever step we are on, God pursues us. "For God would have all men to be saved and to come to the knowledge of the truth."[14] As you read this book, God seeks a response from you. He wants you to take the next step. Will you do it?

Notes
[3] Genesis 1:1
[4] Genesis 1:31
[5] Isaiah 14:12-14
[6] 1 Peter 1:20
[7] Luke 22:42
[8] John 1:29
[9] Galatians 4:4
[10] John 3:6
[11] Ephesians 2:1-5
[12] Hebrews 11:6
[13] Romans 10:17
[14] 1 Timothy 2:4

For Personal Reflection...

1. Various sources for inaccurate messages about the nature of God are discussed in the chapter. Think about the way you may have been impacted by these:

   A The church

   A Our earthly fathers

   A Messages from society

   A Ugliness of sin

   A Unanswered prayers

   A Ignorant comments by parents, others

   A False religions and cults

2. Have you personally believed and embraced all "the Truth from Genesis to Revelation" shared?

3. Are you certain of your personal salvation decision?

4. To what next step on your personal spiritual journey to true holiness do you feel God calling you?

ACT TWO:
BEING CHANGED BY HIM
Changed through
Abiding with Jesus Christ

How the heart is set free to be imbued with all the beauty of God when finally it truly knows Him!

As previously mentioned, the all-consuming, eternal desire of the heart of God is to reproduce in human spirits the beauty of holiness, of His love. So many things work to prevent us truly comprehending His nature and deter us from absolute yielding to His purposes in our lives. But as we cooperate with God and yield to His direction and the "props", Act One: "Knowing God" gradually plays out in our lives. Fully comprehending the true nature of God produces the trust necessary for complete yielding, and transforms the heart into clay in the hands of the potter.[15] Only then can God have full rein to powerfully maximize the life-changing potency of His spirit's presence and working in our lives.

Many illustrations depict the process of changing and beautifying us that God desires to accomplish in our lives. The refining fire that purifies gold. Clay in the potter's hands. An uncut diamond under the jeweler's chisel. I often share

a metaphor with my clients I call "The Mudbath Principle".
I ask them to picture this world as though they were God
looking at it from His infinite perspective. What He sees
as He looks at all we human beings in our struggles here
is a bottomless pit of black, slimy mud which has all of us
trapped and filthy. Everyone of us is sullied with the dirt
and incapable of getting out and getting clean. God compas-
sionately reaches down and lifts us out of the mud. As he
takes His hand and carefully, gently removes the mud that
stains us, incredibly He gradually uncovers a shining, radiant
human being who reflects His image! His image was always
there, just hidden and fouled by the mud of sin that entraps
all of us in Paradise Lost. Once uncovered, that image can
brilliantly impact everything it shines on with the beauty of
God's holiness.

The first thing necessary for God to transform us into His
beauty is for our consuming desire to line up with His. "Seek
ye first the Kingdom of God and His righteousness..."[16] In
the metaphor, relocating to HopeFound requires that we let
go of all the confusing, faulty messages about the purpose
and meaning of life and align our hearts with the reality that
He is everything. "For to me to live is Christ..."[17] As we're
growing to truly know His heart and trust Him the passion
that drives Him becomes the passion that drives us, and we
are able to focus on "Kingdom living." The time and energy
previously spent in building delusional walls of protection to
hide from soul-wounding pain can now be invested cooperatively with God in His character-rebuilding efforts in us.

Once our heart's passion is to mature into a servant prof-
itable to our heavenly Father, the drama of a lifetime has
begun! The God-Man cooperative, symbolized in the metaphor as the Supreme Director and His key cast member,
will be a lifetime symbiosis to transform us into a closer
and closer reflection of Him. As we pro-actively participate

with God's Spirit to accomplish that crucial goal, several key components are necessary to fulfill our God-intended role.

The first and most essential task is to develop an abiding relationship with our Lord. The gospel of John, chapter 15, has profound advice about life-changing relationship with Jesus Christ. "I am the vine and you are the branches. If a man abides in Me, he will bear much fruit; apart from Me you can do nothing...If you abide in Me and My words abide in you, ask whatever you wish, and it will be given you. This is to My Father's glory, that you bear much fruit..."

What does it mean to abide? A good translation is to continually dwell in Jesus. It also means to persevere in remaining in Him. Jesus wants to be our dwelling place, our home, the place from which we draw our strength to go out and face the day. As the vine provides the sap to the branch to grow and bear fruit, Jesus is our vine. We must draw sustenance from continual connection with Him if we are to mature and become fruit-bearing in His Kingdom. Without the sap of His potent Spirit coursing into our souls we are dead and worthless spiritually.

Practically speaking, abiding is accomplished by time spent with our Lord. For Jesus' Spirit's life-changing power to be set free in us we need to open the fountain of our being to Him through deep, intimate communion on a regular basis. In human relationships intimacy happens through communication; we talk, listen, and respond to one another. In our relationship with God, the Spirit talks to us and we listen to Him through his Word, and we talk to Him and respond to Him and He to us through prayer.

Jesus' statement about the absolute necessity of this communion is unequivocal: without it we can do nothing. Yet in our lives as Christians we so easily neglect or even ignore this essential element. We make excuses for not taking the time, making the time. While proclaiming our passionate love for God and His Kingdom, we starve ourselves spiritually and wonder why we're not growing and making an impact for good in His Kingdom. We may even memorize verses extolling the efficacy of the Word in our lives, yet leave the Good Book lying dusty on the shelf.

Satan loves it. To the degree that he can keep us disconnected from our power source he keeps us malnourished and stunted spiritually. In the ageless warfare between him and God, between Good and Evil, he has rendered us crippled, useless non-combatants.

By definition "word" means the essence of, the true reflection of what it stands for. The phrase, the Word of God, immediately calls to mind the written Scriptures. Actually the Word, reflective of the true essence of God, exists in several forms.

The infinite creative power of God was demonstrated and activated through his spoken word as he spoke the universe into existence, as described in Genesis 1.

Jesus has eternally been the true essence of God as the Word; in His incarnation He became that essence in human flesh. "In the beginning was the Word, and the Word was with God, and the Word was God...the Word became flesh and dwelt among us."[18]

In his spoken word and in the Word-made-flesh God has revealed his true nature to us. The written Word is another way in which he does that. It makes the written Word very precious when we realize that it is, like God's spoken word and like Jesus, just as authentic and powerful a literal manifestation of the true essence of God. And we have the privilege to hold it in our hands and read it everyday! As we faithfully expose ourselves to the essence of God in his written Word, the Holy Spirit uses this sacred exposure to transmit into our spirit the very nature of God embedded within that Word. We become increasingly like him! Paul said in Galatians, "For the fruit of the Spirit is love, joy, peace, patience, kindness, goodness, faithfulness, gentleness and self-control."[19] A very accurate description of the character of God, and its available to us!

For the record, let's note what Scripture has to say about itself. "Faith cometh by hearing, and hearing by the Word of God"[20] ..."all Scripture is God-breathed, and is useful for teaching, rebuking, correcting and training in righteousness, so that the man of God may be thoroughly equipped for every good work"[21] ..."the Word of God is quick and powerful and sharper than any two-edged sword, dividing asunder the soul and the spirit, and is a discerner of the thoughts and intents of the heart"[22] ... "I have hidden your Word in my heart that I might not sin against you[23]...I gain understanding from your precepts; therefore I hate every wrong path. Your Word is a lamp to my feet and a light for my path"[24] ... "Like newborn babies, crave pure spiritual milk, so that by it you may grow up in your salvation"[25] ..."Study to show thyself a workman approved by God that needeth not to be ashamed, rightly dividing the Word of truth."[26]

Developing a method for spending time with God in his Word and in prayer that works for you and that you can realistically practice is the foundational building block for maturing spiritually. Christian book stores have multitudes of volumes devoted to this subject, and anyone interested can find lots of helpful advice. Whatever program works for you, make sure it contains several essential components.

A necessary ingredient in devotional time with God is undisturbed quiet to really meditate on his Word and commune in prayer. Let's not trivialize this remarkable privilege we have to relate to the heavenly Father by giving only half-hearted attention to it. While thinking about God, talking about him, and praying to him through-out the day are all components of "abiding", they don't go deep enough. God wants personal, private time with us! Some religious orders have discovered the necessity of isolation and privacy for deep connection with God and conduct retreats where silence is maintained for several days. God speaks in a still, small voice!

While our twentieth century lifestyle is often frenzied and chaotic, we still CHOOSE those things that we make time for and those that we don't. Whatever the sacrifice, no matter how difficult it is to come up with a workable schedule, choose quality time with God. Without it you will languish spiritually. Find a simple technique or plan that structures you for success. An example that works for me is to say first thing in the morning, "Don't' leave the bedroom without it", referring to my quiet time with God. Experiment with various ideas until you find one that works. Expect powerful resistance from Satan. He knows that he will be defeated when God's people really communicate intimately with Him on a regular basis.

I have found that I can create a "God's-presence-zone" in my home by always having my devotional time with him in the same place. After many, many occasions of precious fellowship with him in that old bentwood rocker in the bedroom, just to sit down there takes me immediately into his presence. The world fades away and I find my heart transported into close rapport with my God. While certainly life will not always allow us to be in the same place at the same time to connect with God, it is a worthy goal to pursue.

Studying the Bible in a life-changing, efficacious way requires more than just ritualistic reading of a portion of Scripture daily. We need to meditate on the Word. The word "meditate" means literally to "chew the cud". When a cow chews the cud she brings the same food back into her mouth repeatedly until she has squeezed every bit of nutritious value out of it. Our goal as we come to God's Word is to read and think and reread and re-think until we've "digested" every drop of meaning out of it! And we can claim a wonderful promise in the Word: the Holy Spirit will be our guide in this endeavor! Jesus said to his disciples that after he left the Spirit would come and guide them into all truth.[27] Paul said in 1 Corinthians that the Spirit who searches the deep things of God would teach those spiritual truths to us.[28] Bible study aids can be tremendously helpful, but it is the Spirit of God who will enlighten our spirit with his truth.

A structure that really enriches and improves devotional time is to keep a devotional journal. Date each entry-this helps you track how faithfully you are reading. Read a portion of Scripture and note it in your journal. A procedure I recommend is to read through complete books both Old and New Testament, a portion at a time day-by-day, reading only the portion that time allows you to fully consider each day. After reading a specific portion and meditating on it, write in your journal a response to what you read. This response can be formulated as an outline, a summary, answers to questions such as "who"? "what"? "where"? etc. or any other format that works for you. I have simplified my written response to noting at least one significant truth that I sense God calling to my attention. The final crucial step is the most vital of all. Write a personal application of the truth/s you noted from this Scripture passage. What response does this passage require of you? This is where the rubber meets the road. The value of Bible study and meditation is applying it to our lives and letting God change us through it. No matter how much knowledge we have of what the Bible says, unless it changes us it is meaningless. Many Christians are full of Bible knowledge yet lacking in Godly character and lifestyle.

One last point about the role of God's written Word in our lives: we need to commit it to memory. To refer back to the verse, "I have hidden thy Word in my heart, that I might not sin against thee,"[29] the necessity of knowing the Word if it is going to be beneficial in our lives is clear. We need to be able to think God's thoughts when temptation comes knocking on our door, when life demands a Godly response or Godly wisdom or truth. The immediacy of many situations does not allow getting the Bible and looking for the appro-

Hope Found in Paradise Lost

priate scripture application. Further, we are told to "be ready to give an answer to anyone who asks about the hope that is in you."[30] When a God-given opportunity to share about our faith happens, we need to be ready to give an inspired response. To use a Bible metaphor, a soldier in the army of God needs to have a sharpened sword of the Word ready for battle.

Years ago as a young woman I selected about 20 different key verses from the Bible that addressed various significant spiritual issues. I wrote them on cards and committed them to memory. I could not begin to estimate the number of times those verses have been called to mind over the years by God's spirit as I dealt with a personal situation in my own life or conversed with someone about God. Knowing them well enough to quote them has been invaluable in my efforts to share my faith and convictions with those God brings my way.

Memorizing can be tough, but it is not impossible. Memorize the Word. God's Spirit will help you. Satan will resist your efforts. But "resist the devil and he will flee from you."[31]

The other essential component of a meaningful devotional time with God is prayer. Simply stated, prayer is our talking to God, his responding to us, and our listening to his response. Many of the most important decisions I've ever made or insights I've ever achieved have come through God's clear voice being heard as I've spent time talking to him and listening to him in prayer. As we pour out our hearts to him and open the ears of our spirit to hear his response, he impresses upon us his direction for our lives, his wisdom for the moment.

As previously stated, a prerequisite for this kind of communication with God is quiet, uninterrupted time with him. We will be able to hear the still small voice of God when we have slowed down, cleared our minds of the inconsequential clutter of daily living, communicated well with him, and tuned in spiritually to hear his response. When we create that kind of fertile, receptive condition in our spirit, God is given opportunity to impress on that receptive soil his guidance, his strength, his wisdom for our lives.

Developing a prayer process that allows the deep communion described above to happen is the other prerequisite. We need to figure out HOW to do it! One of Jesus' disciples asked him one day, "Lord, teach us how to pray".[32] Jesus' answer to that disciple's weighty request was, "Say, 'Our Father who art in heaven, hallowed be thy name. Thy kingdom come, thy will be done, on earth as it is in heaven. Give us this day our daily bread. Forgive us our sins as we forgive those who sin against us. Lead us not into temptation, but deliver us from evil." [33](The additional phrase, "For thine is the Kingdom, and the power, and the glory" is not found in original Bible manuscripts). This model prayer that Jesus taught the disciples that day has been referred to as "The Lord's Prayer" throughout Church history, but rightfully should be called "The Disciples' Prayer". I believe the answer Jesus gave those first disciples was literally meant to provide a pattern for prayer for them as well as for us who have followed them in God's Kingdom.

That disciple asked a question all serious followers of Christ have attempted to find an answer to, as we have sought to grow spiritually. I struggled for years to find a meaningful, effective way to pray that would keep me awake and focused, cover the necessary subject matter, and give me a sense of true connection with God. Years ago when I began using the Disciples' Prayer as a literal outline for my prayers, my prayer life became focused, intense, and powerfully life-changing. For those reading this book who may still be in that struggle for meaningful prayer life, I share the method that has benefited me tremendously.

The procedure I use involves speaking each phrase as an introductory comment, and then pouring out my heart in personal conversation with God related to that phrase. Every phrase is given serious consideration. Following is a phrase-by-phrase description of what is discussed in each portion of prayer.

The first several phrases focus my thoughts and emotions on loving, appreciating, and worshipping God.

> **"My Father"** (I choose to say "my" rather than "our", since this is personal prayer). This beginning portion of prayer focuses on the incredible truth that God is my heavenly father. With deep appreciation I describe him as a Father, and glory in the possessive "my": I am his and he is mine.
>
> **"...who art in heaven."** This phrase allows me to acknowledge God as the creator and sovereign ruler of the universe-and yet "my father".
>
> **"Hallowed be thy name."** To hallow is to revere and honor highly. This phrase involves worshipfully speaking many, many words of worship, reverence, and magnification of my wonderful God. "Father, you are worthy of glory, and honor, and reverence, and exaltation and..." I also pray that my life will hallow, or bring honor to, my heavenly Father's name today.

When I have finished this first portion of prayer, my heart is overflowing with deep, worshipful love and appreciation for God my father. The next several phrases involve petitioning God to hear and respond to my requests.

> **"Thy Kingdom come, thy will be done, on earth as it is in heaven."** Here all the concerns in my life and my world that need God's attention are shared with him. I pray

for God's will to be known and accomplished in an ever-widening circle of circumstances addressed, seeking his direction, intervention and help to bring that about. I start with my own heart condition and personal concerns, progress through my marriage and family, and continue through career, church, ministry, and eventually issues of concern country-wide and world-wide. Throughout this segment of prayer an uppermost concern is that, in all the circumstances of life addressed, God's Kingdom purposes would be advanced. This portion of prayer is not a selfishly motivated "I want..." list. The heart of this segment is impassioned pleading for <u>God's</u> wants to be accomplished.

"Give me today my daily bread." Praying for God's help and provision for the demands of life today, e.g. protection from harm, needed strength, pragmatic provision of necessary things, etc., falls into this segment of prayer. The acknowledgement of my utter dependence on God "just for today," as the old song says, flows out of these petitions.

"Forgive me my sins, as I forgive those who sin against me." My response to my sin and to those who sin against me is brought before God here. First I pray for a sensitive spirit to discern my own sin, and then seek God's forgiveness for that sin, vowing not to repeat it again, by his grace. This phrase also makes it very clear that God uses the litmus-test of our ability to forgive others as indicative of our purity of heart, and expects us to deal with the sin of unforgiveness before expecting forgiveness from him. Keep in mind that forgiveness is not primarily an emotion, but a <u>choice</u> to let go of bitterness, anger, resentment, and the right to hold that person in my debt for what he/she did, and even to execute punishment on them, subtle or otherwise. Over time, being faithful to that commitment to forgive changes the way we feel about that offending person. We cannot program our emotions, but God insists that we make the choice to forgive.

"Lead me not into temptation, but deliver me from evil". Everyday, all day, every Christian wages a battle with Satan for control of his mind, his emotions, his behavior, and ultimately his spirit's wellbeing. It is essential to seek the Spirit's power in overcoming temptation, whatever form it will take in this day. If I am aware of particular temptations that this day will hold or that I am prone to, I address them specifically. I also pray to be kept away from the places where temptation lurks, seeking to ambush me. I claim the power of the Holy Spirit in me to overcome evil. I ask for a perfect day.

Though the last phrase, **"For thine is the Kingdom, and the power, and the glory"**, is not in original manuscripts, I nevertheless choose to close my prayer time with this phrase. It is an appropriate ending to this time of communion with my Father because it transitions me out of prayer and into my day with a focus on the sovereignty and power of God. What better perspective could I have as I begin my day?

One additional aspect of my prayer experience which is very gratifying is quoting Scripture back to God. Through-out my prayer-time I interject verses that pertain to that portion of my prayer, and agree with God by speaking his thoughts about the subject. An example might be, "May the words of my mouth and the meditation of my heart be pleasing in your sight, O Lord, my rock and my redeemer."[34] Or I may claim the promise, "…because the One who is in you is greater than the one who is in the world (Satan)."[35] There is something very legitimate about speaking God's written word back to him in prayer.

An absolutely essential element in God's desire to change us into His image is that we pursue a spirit-nurturing, abiding relationship with Him through time spent in Scripture meditation, memorization, and prayer. He won't make us do it; it's up to us. Do it.

Notes
[15] Romans 9:21
[16] Matthew 6:33
[17] Philippians 1:21
[18] John 1:1,14
[19] Galatians 5:22,23
[20] Romans 10:17
[21] 11 Timothy 3:16
[22] Hebrews 4:12
[23] Psalms 119:11
[24] Psalms 119 104,105
[25] 1 Peter 2:2
[26] 11 Timothy 2:15
[27] John 16:13
[28] 1 Corinthians 2:10
[29] Psalms 119:11
[30] 1 Peter 3:15
[31] James 4:7
[32] Luke 11:1
[33] Matthew 6:9-13
[34] Psalms 19:14

[35] 1 John 4:4b

For Personal Reflection...

1. To what degree are you like a branch, tapping into Christ, the source of your spiritual growth and fruit-bearing?

   ⋏ How effective and regular is your personal Bible study?

   ⋏ Is your prayer life genuine, effective communion with God? Consider trying the "Lord's Prayer" format described in this chapter.

   ⋏ How much of God's Word do you have "hidden in your heart"? Consider beginning a regimen of determined memorization of Scripture.

2. Review your life since your salvation. Can you recognize areas of growth and change? Are you still growing and changing? If not, why not?

ACT TWO:
"BEING CHANGED BY HIM
Changed through a
Renewed Mind

As the drama of my life plays out on the stage in HopeFound, Act Two is "Being Changed By Him." God wants to change us into His image. Choosing God means choosing change. It is inevitable and necessary for His further plans for us. Besides an abiding relationship with God, His Word tells us about several other life-changing processes he uses in our journey of spiritual maturation.

A very necessary trait for continuing growth is being able to think God's thoughts about all aspects of life. The abiding relationship with God described in the previous chapter provides the opportunity to know His Word and receive the Holy Spirit's help in understanding His truth provided therein. Yet there is a hidden mental process at work which can sabotage our ability to apply God's truth to our lives. Often, co-existing with God's revealed truth in our minds are powerfully motivating contradictory beliefs which covertly urge us to act according to their version of "truth".

The beliefs we embrace will define our choices and thus our character, and the degree to which we live out God's will for us. Contemporary psychologists have identified the importance of our embraced beliefs in motivating our behavior, but God said it first. His Word has many things to say about the power of our thoughts . I'll reference just a few of them here. "As a man thinketh in his heart (mind) so is he."[36] "Above all else, guard your heart (mind) for it is the wellspring of life."[37] "We demolish arguments and every pretension that sets itself up against the knowledge of God, and we take captive every thought to make it obedient to Christ."[38] "Let this mind be in you which was also in Christ Jesus..."#[39] "For out of the heart come evil thoughts, murder, adultery, sexual immorality, theft, false testimony, slander..."[40]

Many more verses could be referenced, but perhaps the most clear statement of the mind-behavior connection is found in Romans 12:2. "Don't be conformed to this world, but be transformed by the renewing of your mind, in order to demonstrate the good and perfect and acceptable will of God." This verse teaches tremendously significant truth about being changed by God. Let's take it apart and see what it says to us.

There is a promise in this verse that we <u>can</u> demonstrate, or consistently practice, God's good, perfect, acceptable will for our lives. That promise is conditioned on our first accomplishing that which is described in the first two phrases of the verse. "Don't be conformed to this world" means not to allow our life experiences in Paradise Lost to mold or shape us to reflect the beliefs, values, and practices of this ungodly fallen world in which we live. How do we not do that? The next phrase says, "but be transformed by the renewing of your mind". "Renew" implies that something new replaces something already in existence. God's Word is saying that replacing the world's lies with His truth will transform us from conformity to the world's practices to living out His perfect will for our lives. What an awesome hope!

In my counseling practice, helping my clients work through this process of replacing the world's lies with God's truth is essential to any permanent change. What psychologists have come to understand, and what God our creator has always known, is that our thoughts create our emotions, which then drive our responses. We tend to think that our feelings cause our behavior, but underlying our feelings is a core belief or conscious thought that provoked the feeling. To change behavior we have to first change our underlying thoughts. That's what God said in several different Scriptures already quoted. A simple illustration might be helpful.

If a woman's husband forgets to give her a Valentine card, she may think, "His forgetfulness shows that I am really unimportant to him." Her emotional response to this thought will then be feelings of hurt, and/or resentment or worthlessness. Consequently she may react negatively with a behavior such as withdrawing, uttering an angry comment, trying to please him more, or whatever her programmed reaction to this feeling may be. However, when her husband forgets to give her a Valentine card, she may instead say to herself, "I know he's been really busy; he shows me he values me in ways other than cards," or perhaps, "Though he doesn't treat me as of much value to him, I know that my true value comes from God." The emotion created by those thoughts will be entirely different. She will still be disappointed, but without the accompanying feelings of resentment, hurt, or worthlessness. She will then be free to seek an unconditionally loving response to him, which may include sharing her feelings about his forgetfulness.

This brief scenario illustrates the principle that thoughts drive feelings which drive behavior. I am not suggesting that we are powerless to choose a loving response in the face of hurtful feelings. By God's grace we certainly can and should do so. But feelings are Satan's playground. He loves an opportunity to stir up and then capitalize on negative emotions such as those described above to elicit a self-protective, selfish reaction. This is one of his most successful ploys in seducing even mature Christians to override their commitment to Christ-like behavior. When we feel hurt or threatened, we are most vulnerable to yield to a self-centered reaction rather than a loving, other-centered response.

Regardless of feelings, we are always responsible to respond in love; if we don't it is sin. Thinking God's thoughts instead of Satan's mistruths is a powerful way to short-circuit Satan's efforts to create an emotional vulnerability which entices us to yield to his voice rather than God's. It is necessary for emotional objectivity and for the freedom to make choices based on God's will rather than a selfish or self-protective reaction. Since this is true, identifying and dispelling our beliefs contradictory to God's truth is critical.

One source of emotion-laden misbeliefs is our childhood misinterpretations of hurtful life experiences. As previously discussed in the chapter, "Why Walls of Protection in Paradise Lost?", right from birth, life here in Paradise Lost always involves imperfect parenting, often painful life experiences, injustice, and soul-wounding unmet needs. As we attempt to make sense of the messages seemingly implied in these circumstances, these unfolding life experiences coupled with our individual makeup lead each of us to our own distinct set of beliefs, some of which are distortions or contradictions of God's truth. We may believe lies such as "God is uncaring and unapproachable," "I'm a worthless loser," "I have to be perfect to be loved by God and others," "the most important thing in life is money (power, sex, pleasure, success, happiness...)," etc.

Identifying the particular lies that living in Paradise Lost has taught us and replacing those lies with God's truth is one critical step to "be transformed by the renewing of your mind." These are typically unconscious level core beliefs that we are completely unaware of, and might even deny believing if confronted with them. Yet they covertly drive every nuance of our behavior, hidden though they are.

Rooting out these mistruths requires revisiting the past with the intention to honestly appraise the way in which our needs were or were not met by our parents and through other significant life events and how we "explained" or interpreted those unmet needs. Thoughtfully reviewing all the various circumstances of our childhood, such as relationship dynamics in our family of origin, our parents' parenting style, school experiences, significant life events such as deaths, moves, serious illness, family crisis, etc., may bring awareness of childhood experiences that led to what some psychologists call "stinkin' thinkin.'" Appendix A contains many typical "stinkin' thinkin'" distorted beliefs that hurting children internalize during childhood as a result of their inaccurate childish explanations for patterns of unmet needs.

Typically the need for discerning these false core beliefs is not recognized until life begins to unravel in some way: your marriage is failing, your career development is stagnating, depression has gripped you with black despair, anxiety haunts your days, or some other deterrent prevents the fulfillment you want from life. Something seems to be working against your ability to live the abundant, victorious life promised by God. What may be at work is these unconscious level beliefs from the past. Once established during childhood in a person's mind, these distorted messages will continue to be reinforced throughout life as he/she looks at life through the lens of that perception and sees what she believes. Misreading and misinterpreting his life experiences according to his preconceived beliefs, he thus responds incorrectly and often sinfully to them.

Karen* came to my office several years ago, saying her life was a mess and she needed to be "fixed." She was separated from her husband, having problems at work, struggling with anxiety continually, and exhibiting symptoms related to anxiety disorder. What struck me immediately as I talked with Karen was how often she made demeaning, self-deprecating comments. Though she was attractive, articulate, and likeable, her image of herself was extremely negative. As she shared her history with me, she described parents who were very career-focused perfectionists whom she found impossible to please. It gradually became clear that she had internalized a message of inferiority, inadequacy and shame that plagued her everyday of her life.

These negative messages caused her to expect failure from herself, blame herself unrealistically, and worry excessively about everything. "Renewing her mind" required that she consciously recognize the underlying lie from childhood that she was shamefully inferior in every way, and replace it with God's truth that she is of great worth because she was made in His image, for His purposes, and is indeed "fearfully and wonderfully made".[41] As her feelings of inadequacy and fear of failure were gradually replaced with a realistic sense of her own worth as a child of God, she became increasingly able to respond in healthy ways to relationships and life circumstances. Setting boundaries with her husband's thoughtless, disrespectful treatment of her led to a new, healthier dynamic between them, and eventually to restoration of her marriage. While she still struggles with anxiety occasionally, it is a minor issue in her life today.

A couple came in for marriage counseling, struggling over tensions in their relationship caused primarily by his frequent emotional withdrawal and threats to leave, whenever he perceived her to be critical or neglectful of him. She protested that he often misread her feelings of true affection for him, and she then became so discouraged she quit trying. His history revealed that his parents divorced when he was just an infant, and his father disappeared from his life. His mother devoted herself to a series of live-in relationships over the years, but none of the men ever married her or took any serious interest in being a father to him. As we probed for his response to this pattern in his life he brokenly acknowledged that he felt deeply hurt by his mother's neglect and the indifference these men showed to him. He realized that he came to believe that people can't be trusted and will always let you down. His response then-as well as in his marriage-was to protect himself from the pain of abandonment by not making an emotional commitment to anyone. Discovering this core belief underlying his pattern of relationship sabotage was the first step in becoming free to trust and love.

These stories illustrate the power of core beliefs to unconsciously control behavior. It should be noted that, while I have called these core beliefs "lies," they actually were very true in the childhood experiences of these persons. They become lies when they are generalized to all of life and "haunt" later life happenings with the same dynamic as experienced in the past, whether or not it is presently true.

False core beliefs created by our personal interpretations of the meaning of life experiences here in Paradise Lost need to be replaced with God's truth. The thoughtful investigative process described earlier usually unearths these misbeliefs. Additionally, talking about and reliving childhood memories that contain some kind of emotional pain and seeking to grasp how you interpreted those experiences as a child often reveals previously unrecognized false core beliefs. (A warning: if your childhood was full of intense physical or emotional pain, this investigative process should be conducted with the help and support of a professional therapist). Once false core beliefs are identified a very helpful procedure is to write out the "lie" on a 3' x 5' card, then write on the back side of the card a "truth" statement from God's Word, either a principle or a verse. Life circumstances will still trigger you to believe the lie, but repeatedly reviewing and claiming the truth while denying the lie will gradually create the "renewed mind" described in Romans 12:2.

Another source of false beliefs is the current society of which we are a part. The world we live in pummels us continually with both implicit and overt messages totally contradictory to God's truth revealed in His Word. As previously discussed, the entertainment industry, the media, the political and governmental machine, are all sources of information that can subtly influence and even alter our beliefs, while all the while we still believe we have a strong Christian value system. Sometimes the world's lie can come in the advice of a trusted, well-meaning friend. The varying sources of deception are as numerous as Satan's many cunning techniques of temptation. These messages impressed on our belief systems by our culture are the cause of many sinful choices that seemingly "good Christians" make, unconsciously being directed by beliefs only vaguely acknowledged, if at all.

Consider the classic illustration of the frog placed in cold water and then having the heat turned on, who boils to death unalarmed and unaware of the killing heat destroying him, because of the seductive, gradual change taking place. That illustration applies perfectly to our belief systems. The killing heat of worldly lies stealthily destroys the truth through which God seeks to direct our lives, and the result is sin, the death of God's intended good for us. Illustrations abound from current moral battlegrounds: abortion vs. sanctity of life, homosexuality vs. heterosexuality, sexual purity vs. sexual experimentation, seductive dress vs. modesty, responsible money management vs. credit card debt, Sunday worship vs. recreational pursuits, etc. In the warfare between God and Satan, the battle for the mind is the decisive site where victory is won or lost .

We need to subject every thought to the scrutiny of God's Word. "...Take captive every thought to make it obedient to Christ."[42] Regardless of the supposedly authoritative or trustworthy source of the thought or the information, God's Word has to be the litmus test for truth.

Romans 12:2 promises that we can consistently practice the will of God as we follow the formula laid out in the verse. First, "Do not be conformed to this world..." Pursuing an abiding relationship with Jesus Christ through study and memorization of His Word, prayer, and commitment to godliness produces the knowledge of the truth and the desire, commitment, and power to do right. Second, "...but be transformed by the renewing of your mind..." Discerning our personal underlying false core beliefs and society's Satanic deceptions and replacing them with the truth we're learning as we abide with Him is another necessary component. Finally, "..in order to demonstrate the good and perfect and acceptable will of God." The culminating action is the Spirit-empowered choice to follow God's revealed truth over any other source, regardless of feelings, pressures, opinions of others, etc.

On the stage of my life in HopeFound, The dramatic Act Two: "Being Changed by Him" plays out as I abide with him through consistent study of his word and prayer, as I keep a renewed mind through continually clarifying God's truth versus deception from whatever source, and as I call upon the Holy Spirit's strength to act in obedience to His truth and do His will, regardless of feelings or any other alluring influence. One other significant force influences my maturation in HopeFound, which we will discuss in the next chapter.

*Fictitious name

Notes
[36] Proverbs 23:7
[37] Proverbs 4:23
[38] 11 Corinthians 10:5
[39] Philippians 2:5
[40] Matthew 15:19
[41] Psalms 139:14
[42] 11 Corinthians 10:5

For Personal Reflection...

1. As you review childhood experiences and the "Stinkin' Thinkin'" list of false core beliefs, consider whether you believe any false messages internalized in your past. If so, how is that belief interfering with God's purposes in your life? What Truth from God's Word do you need to claim to overcome this false belief?

2. Watch for situations in your life that illustrate the dynamic that thoughts create feelings that cause behavioral responses, as discussed in the chapter. Replace a false belief with God's truth and experience the change in your feelings and response.

3. Thoughtfully consider whether the beliefs and value system promoted by this world and Satan have influenced your convictions and behavior. What change in thinking/belief and behavior do you need to make?

ACT TWO:
"BEING CHANGED BY HIM"
Changed through Suffering

Nobody wants to suffer. Suffering is the anathema of our souls. Yet remarkably the Bible says, "Count it all joy when you fall into various trials and testings..."[43]

Suffering is perhaps God's most effective technique for changing us, and the one most misunderstood and hated. Starting with people in the Old Testament such as Joseph, David, Daniel, etc., and continuing down through human history we find countless stories of people who became awesome tools in God's hands through personal suffering. Rarely does an individual make a significant spiritual impact in his world whose life story does not contain adversity.

Why do we have to suffer to become more spiritually mature? To go back to the beginning, Adam and Eve lived in a perfect garden and had a perfect relationship with God and each other. Sounds pretty spiritually mature to me. Couldn't get much better, right? Then sin entered the human experience and Adam and Eve's life, along with ours, was forever changed. The devastating change that took place in their hearts with sin's arrival was selfishness. Because they lost so much, they became focused on finding ways to get those things back. That continues to be the core motivation that drives each of us as their descendants today: life is about protecting myself from the pain of unmet needs. All sin evolves from this obsession with self-protection, played upon by Satan, the world's value system, and the natural desires of the flesh.[44] Our unique set of life circumstances and inherent traits produce our particular soul-wounds and "style of sinning." The wall-building process in the HopeFound metaphor depicts this fixation on self-protection.

The most profound change that God wants us to experience is to break the hold that this obsessive self-interest has on our heart. Self-centeredness is the opposite of unconditional love, and thus is absolutely contrary to His nature that He wants to impart to us. The problem is that we have a very difficult time recognizing this self-centered core motivation. We see life through the grid of our fears, needs, and desires and think that our behavior is reasonable and even godly. "The heart is deceitful above all things and beyond cure; who can understand it?"[45] Though God may be able to get us to recognize specific sins and perhaps overcome them, some other sin driven by self-protection will always be present.

What is needed is a transformation in this undercover, controlling, yes, even life-dominating force. God will have no other gods before Him. He insists that the desire of our hearts be focused on Him and Him alone. Breaking this vicious hold of self-interest on our heart is suffering's intended outcome. It is the deepest-level change of all, the most resistant to surrender, and the most profoundly life-changing when consummated. Touching the very core of our being and changing what drives us from that inner place is the noble cause for which God allows suffering to plague our souls. Nothing else in human experience seems to be able to change us in this essential way.

I love the song, "The Touch of the Master's Hand." It presents an allegorical story of a master violin virtuoso and the priceless violin he created. As he picks up the violin and touches the bow to the strings he produces matchlessly beautiful music only he is capable of producing. Why? Because as the creator of the violin he knows better than anyone else how to make beautiful music with it. As he draws the bow across the strings, he knows exactly how much pressure to apply to each string and at what point to elicit the most pure sound from the instrument. So it is with our God. As He draws the bow of His personal involvement with us across the strings of our lives, as our creator He knows best how much stress to apply, where, and for how long to produce the clear, beautiful music of a godly soul.

Suffering is not the enemy of mankind but our greatest friend. It does not reflect God's indifference to our plight but His greatest efforts in our behalf. It should not be resented or avoided but received with rejoicing. Through suffering our worst spiritual enemy, self-obsession, can be put to death.

My experience in the loss of my marriage perfectly illustrates this truth. As a young wife and mother I saw myself as unselfishly investing my life in pursuit of God's purposes. I did not recognize that co-existing with that motivation were deeper needs driven by soul-wounds from the past for unconditional love, security, and significance, and those goals drove even my spiritual pursuits. To some degree I was motivated to be a great Christian so that I would be loved, secure, and significant. Competing with my genuine love for God as the prime motivator of my life was this self-centered focus which produced my feverish wall-building efforts. As long as I could cling to the delusion that I could make life as I wanted it to be, that was a powerful, driving motivation of my life. That delusion had to die to set me free to pursue God's truer, greater purposes with an undivided heart.

Fortunately we human beings are usually not so foolish as to continue to pursue something proven to be unattainable. When harsh reality proved to me that walls of protection are non-existent in Paradise Lost, I gave up on that meaningless pursuit. Deep emotional pain and loss was the death-wielding weapon that demolished my self-centered obsession with wall-building by killing hope of safety in Paradise Lost. It was a soul-wrenching loss because that belief had comforted, consumed, and sustained me.

Broken-hearted and terrified, I looked frantically to God for some other source of safety in this painful place. And in that season of intense vulnerability, my desperate need focused my attention on Him as never before. It was then He was able to impart to me the wonderful truths portrayed in the HopeFound metaphor. Paul says it so well in 2 Corinthians 12:9,10: "But He (the Lord) said to me, 'My grace is sufficient for you, for my power is made perfect in weakness.' Therefore I will boast all the more gladly about my weaknesses, so that Christ's power may rest on me. This is why, for Christ's sake, I delight in weaknesses, in insults, in hardships, in persecutions, in difficulties. For when I am weak, then I am strong." Sadly, God often has to become our "last hope" before we finally fling ourselves on Him for meaning and safety in life.

The principle of suffering as preparation for powerful service is a repeating theme throughout Scripture, illustrated by many Old Testament stories. Abraham was asked to leave his homeland and go to a faraway place before becoming the father of the Hebrew nation; Joseph suffered immensely in preparation for being God's human instrument to save that same Hebrew nation; Moses was cast out of Pharaoh's court and spent 40 years on the back side of the desert before leading the children of Israel out of captivity; as Job processed his severe suffering he came to know God in a deeper way and to yield absolutely to His sovereign rule in his life; David suffered military persecution, moral failure, and loss of loved ones in his preparation for royal leadership; Jonah languished in the belly of a whale three days to break his stubborn spirit and prepare him to minister to Nineveh; Daniel was separated from his family and homeland and his faith was tested by temptations of an ungodly culture before his heroic walk with the lions. These few examples are only a sampling of the many Old testament illustrations of preparatory growth through suffering.

The New Testament has much to say about suffering. Jesus talked more about suffering than He did about heaven or hell. He said that anyone who would follow Him must take up his cross,[46] that whoever wants to save his life will lose it, but whoever loses his life for Christ's sake will find it.[47] In the Beatitudes He said that blessed are those who mourn, and those who are persecuted and insulted because of the Son of Man.[48] In the Vine and Branches metaphor in John 15 He said that every branch in Him that bears fruit will be pruned in order to bear more fruit. [49]He prophesied that, as His servants, the disciples would be persecuted as He was persecuted.[50] During His last supper in the upper room the last evening of His human life, in the most intimate conversation recorded in the Bible between Jesus and His disciples, Jesus said "In this world you will have trouble. But take heart! I have overcome this world."[51] Jesus consistently warned the disciples that life as a follower of Christ would not be easy, but would involve persecution, suffering and distress. They did not want to hear it. We followers of Christ today do not want to hear it.

Numerous other New Testament Scriptures weave together a vivid picture of suffering as an essential ingredient in believers' lives. Several have already been referenced in the chapter, "Scriptural Foundation for the Metaphor", but bear repeating in this context. "Consider it pure joy, my brothers, whenever you face trials of many kinds, because you know that the testing of your faith develops perseverance. Perseverance must finish its work so that you may be mature and complete, not lacking anything.".[52] "...Now for a little while you may have had to suffer grief in all kinds of trials. These have come so that your faith-of greater worth than gold, which perishes even though refined by fire-may be proved genuine and may result in praise, glory and honor when Jesus Christ is revealed."[53] "Therefore, since Christ suffered in His body, arm yourselves also with the same attitude, because he who has suffered in his body is done with sin. As a result, he does not live the rest of his earthly life for evil human desires, but rather for the will of God."[54] "Dear friends, do not be surprised at the painful trial you are suffering, as though something strange were happening to you. but rejoice that you participate in the sufferings of Christ, so that you may be overjoyed when His glory is revealed."[55] "Not only so, but we also rejoice in our sufferings, because we know that suffering produces perseverance; perseverance, character; and character, hope. And hope does not disappoint us because God has poured out His love into our hearts by the Holy Spirit whom He has given us."[56] "...God disciplines us for our good that we may share in His holiness. No discipline seems pleasant at the time, but painful. Later on, however, it produces a harvest of righteousness and peace for those who have been trained by it."[57]

The overwhelming conclusion we can draw from these verses is that through suffering God's highest desires for His children can be achieved. Suffering builds godly character and maturity in believers, strengthens our faith, destroys the grip of sin, brings glory to Christ, creates a focus on doing the will of God, reproduces God's love in us, and ultimately yields a "harvest of righteousness".

God's Word establishes two reassuring boundaries placed on our experience of suffering. Roman 8:28 says "And we knows that in all things God works for the good of those who love Him, who have been called according to His purpose". This verse declares that God only allows life circumstances, including suffering, on the stage of our lives when He can use them to accomplish His "good" eternal purposes. God is not indifferent or inattentive to the distress of His children. He deeply feels our pain. If God allows it, it is only because He intends to use it. That's a promise. There is no such thing as wasted pain in HopeFound. Given the deep compassion that Jesus exhibited for the suffering of human kind, it makes sense that the only reason He would allow us to suffer would be to fulfill a higher purpose in our lives. However, it is not a given that suffering will always result in these marvelous outcomes. Satan's purposes are that it would reap a harvest of spiritual wreckage in our lives. Note that this is a promise for "...those who love Him, who have been called according to His purpose." When we are dedicated to living according to His purposes, He orchestrates every life experience to enable that promise.

Another wonderful reassurance is that God can be trusted to handle our suffering in ways consistent with His character. He promises that He is watching over our lives very attentively, and will never allow us to be tested beyond our endurance. 1 Corinthians 10:13 says, "No temptation has seized you except what is common to man. And God is faithful; he will not let you be tempted beyond what you can bear. But when you are tempted, he will also provide a way out so that you can stand up under it." Like the analogy of the jeweler cutting the precious stone to set free the brilliance within, He has to know what the limit of the stone's resilience is in order to stop chiseling at just the right moment. He has to know just how much pressure to apply, what angle to use, how many cuts to make, just how far he can go to intensify the brilliance of the stone without destroying it. Our God knows exactly where that point lies in our souls. He has promised He will never allows life circumstances that push us past that point. His purpose is always the release of His brilliant image within, never senseless suffering.

The Bible also makes it clear that God never tempts us to sin. James 1:13 says, "When tempted, no one should say, 'God is tempting me.' For God cannot be tempted by evil, nor does he tempt anyone..." God tests us by allowing difficult, challenging circumstances in our lives, but He never presents sin as a desirable choice or encourages us to pursue it. I have been amazed on a number of occasions when a client has asked me if God brought their adulterous love partner into their lives to tempt them or "make them happy." How absolutely contrary to the very nature of God!

As a therapist many of my clients come to counseling because of intense suffering in their lives. Often their stories have illustrated this profound principle of change through suffering.

> *Carol came to my office for help in over-coming depression that had settled on her two years before, after her 27-year-old son's suicide, and continued to hold her in its grip. They had been a strong, godly family who were active in their church and very close to each other. She had been a stay-at-home Mom who invested herself intensely in her family, and felt that she knew all three of her children well. Her son had relocated to a new city after graduating from college to take a job, and so they had lost the frequent contact they had previously had. When he committed suicide Carol felt an overwhelming sense of guilt that somewhere along the way she had failed him as a Mom, that she had "missed something," that in retrospect she should have known something was wrong. She was convinced that if she had been the mother she should have been he would not have committed suicide.

> In the process of dealing with her unre-solved grief, Carol gradually discovered things about herself of which she was previ-ously unaware. She discovered that because

of a soul-wound of deep inferiority she had become a perfectionist, determined to prove to God and the world that she was of worth because she could do everything better than anyone else. Her perfectionism had become the source of her worth and her God. She lived everyday to serve the God of perfectionism, and she expected this God to reward her with her heart's desires. She had been successful most of her life in this pursuit, until her son's suicide. His death declared to her that she was not perfect but terribly flawed, because in her eyes she had failed as a mother, her highest calling. Even more devastating than the loss of her son was the loss of her sense of worth through perfectionism, and the security she had felt in using it to program and control her world. In HopeFound metaphor terminology, her delusional wall of protection, strengthened mightily by feverish perfectionism, had fallen in shambles around her feet.

As Carol dealt with the soul-wound of inferiority and the accompanying coping strategy of perfectionism, she gradually internalized the truth that her worth was in recognizing God's unique design in her and His love and value for her. She was able to let go of the unattainable demand that she prove her worth by being a perfect mother who could magically, through her power, prevent any bad thing from happening in her family. As she gave up on the delusion of that kind of power and responsibility, she discovered the joyous freedom of just being a tool in the hands of a mighty God. For the first time it was not about her worth but it was "all about Him." Because of this dramatic shift in perspective, she was not only able to resolve her grief over her son's suicide but also to pursue "Kingdom living" with enthusiasm and focus.

The multi-faceted plot of Act Two: "Being Changed by Him" is a very complex, exciting portion of the drama of our life in HopeFound. It involves participation with God in an abiding relationship, transformation through a renewed mind, and being changed through suffering. Sometimes subtle, sometimes stunningly intense, the action builds toward readiness for the final, climactic Act Three: "Being Used By Him". But Act three is not a given. Only to the degree that we allow God to change us into His image can this highest, crowning act play out on the stage of our lives.

Notes
[43] James 1:2, KJV
[44] 1 John 2:16
[45] Jeremiah 17:9
[46] Matthew 16:24
[47] Matthew 16:25
[48] Matthew 5:3-11
[49] John 15:2
[50] John 15:20
[51] John 16:33
[52] James 1:2-4
[53] 1 Peter 1:6,7
[54] 1 Peter 4:1,2
[55] 1 Peter 4:12, 13
[56] Romans 5:3-5
[57] Hebrews 12:10b,11

For Personal Reflection...

1. Thoughtfully consider your life experiences of loss and your spiritual response to them. How were you changed spiritually by them? Did they cause a deeper focus on God's purposes, or an intensified self-centered approach to life?

2. Is there an area of suffering in your life today where you need to let go and trust God's sovereignty? Can you apply the concept of God's boundaries on suffering to this situation?

3. Reread the several Scriptures quoted that address suffering as a source of spiritual maturity. Choose at least one to memorize and incorporate into your life.

ACT THREE: "BEING USED BY HIM"

Just as in a play the plot and all the sub-plots and the building momentum of interaction between the characters culminates in the final act, so it is in the drama played out in our lives in HopeFound. Every experience in life that is part of "Act One: Knowing God," and "Act Two: Being Changed by Him" is meant to culminate in the pinnacle "Act Three: Being Used by Him." I am not suggesting that being used by God only comes at the end of our life. But regardless of our season of life, being used by God in the most potent, powerful ways only comes at the end of ourselves, when knowing Him, being changed by Him, and being used by Him are paramount to us. Every thought I think, every move I make, every breath I breathe, everything I feel, every action I take, every motive I honor-EVERYTHING needs to be submitted willingly and gratefully to His intentions, not mine. "...So that now, as always, Christ will be exalted in my body...for the me to live is Christ."[58] As that is true in our lives, God's highest calling for us to become useful tools in His hands can be fulfilled.

God created mankind for relationship, for dynamic, productive interaction. Beginning with the creation of Adam and Eve, every monumental occurrence between God and humankind has been a *God-man cooperative*. As He created the first human beings, our ancestral parents Adam and Eve, the Bible says God stamped them with His image.[59] We are in our essence the first God-man cooperative. In the Garden of Eden He walked with Adam and Eve and they worked with Him to tend His garden: God-man cooperative. Saving the human race from extinction through building an ark with Noah... telling the world about himself through the Hebrew nation... writing the Word, both Old Testament and New Testament, through inspiring human writers. All these are examples of the God-man cooperative, God's chosen means of fulfilling His purposes in the human race.

Unquestionably the pinnacle example of the God-man cooperative is Jesus Christ. God-made-man through the Spirit's impregnation of Mary. The God-man dying both physically and spiritually and being raised by God's spirit to fulfill the highest-ever purpose of God, the redemption of humankind's sin-damaged soul. The incarnation of the Word as Jesus Christ is an incomprehensible, mind-boggling God-man cooperative. Since Jesus' return to heaven the Holy Spirit has continued this mode as He indwells believers to transform and empower us. Another God-man cooperative! The concept of the universal church (all believers) as the body of Christ perfectly illustrates the God-man cooperative. As God indwells our flesh through His Spirit, we become the body of Christ!! As a popular contemporary Christian song says, "We are His body..." He does His work on earth through us. Believers individually and corporately as His church are the ultimate, final God-man cooperative. God's desire is to use believers to complete all His magnificent intentions for the remainder of all time. God's absolute holy power is the guarantee of success for every God-man effort He plans for us. All He needs from us is our availability. Sadly, we limit His success in His great plans for using us when we focus on our weaknesses and perceived limitations instead of His strength and limitless power. Our ability to do remarkable things in the Kingdom of God is limited only by how big we perceive our God to be.

God had our "work assignments" already planned in eternity past before we were even born. "For we are God's workmanship, created in Christ Jesus *to do good works*, which God prepared in advance for us to do."[60] "All the days ordained for me were written in your (God's) book before one of them came to be."[61] "Before I formed you in the womb I knew you, before you were born I set you apart; I appointed you as a prophet to the nations [62](or preacher, or homemaker, or doctor, or missionary, or businessman...) "It was He (Jesus Christ) who gave some to be apostles, some to be prophets, some to be evangelists, and some to be pastors and teachers, *to prepare God's people for works of service,* so that the body of Christ may be built up..."[63]

Being used by God is an immense, even infinite concept. Sometimes we narrowly define being used by God as those who are called to some significant position or role in the Christian community. But being used by God doesn't begin with what we do but who we are. When we have a heart that loves God above all else and our character reflects Him, every moment of our lives can transmit His goodness and love and righteousness into the people, places, and circumstances where we live. Galatians 5:22,23 says "The fruit of the Spirit is love, joy, peace, patience, kindness, goodness, faithfulness, gentleness, and self-control..." God uses that essence of Himself in us to accomplish His intricate, infinite will here on planet earth, and ultimately to accomplish His greatest passion, reproducing His holy love throughout His creation.

In the conversation with His disciples held on His last evening with them, Jesus said that He came to glorify and do the will of God the Father, and that was to be their purpose as well. Usefulness to God will always be defined by whether we obey Him and He receives glory. Scripture says, "So whether you eat or drink or whatever you do, do it all for the glory of God."[64]

As previously noted, Jesus said the greatest commandment was to love the Lord your God and to love your neighbor as yourself. Usefulness to God is also defined by whether or not we truly love. The over-riding characteristics which make our lives useful to God are that He is glorified and that His love is lived out through us. This description is much more sweeping than the idea that only preachers and missionaries and musicians and Sunday School teachers and evangelists can claim to be "used by God". A bed-ridden cripple can glorify God through His attitude and his loving responses in the midst of his disease. A criminal saved by grace can minister the love of God right there in his jail cell. Chuck Colson certainly proved that. A business man can glorify God through the integrity with which he conducts his affairs.

There is no limitation on ways that God's children can be useful to Him. Not age, not race, not place, not vocation, not talents, not health, not wealth, not personality, not appearance. As we allow the beauty of who God is to be reproduced in our flesh, whatever the circumstances of our lives, by our very existence we are exceedingly useful to Him. For whenever we live that way, God always receives the glory as His holiness and love are reflected to a watching world.

The litmus test of our usefulness to God is His receiving the glory as His image is replicated through our lives. Unless our efforts yield this result, the Bible describes them as "wood, hay, and straw"[65] which are of no worth and burn up when tested by fire. How much work done in the name of God which looks great and may even appear to be very fruitful has the underlying motivation of self-glorification, not God's glory? That effort is worthless to God and is symbolically burned up.

Given this definitive criteria for usefulness to God, His glorification as He is reflected in our lives, there are several very significant assignments God has given us to fulfill both individually as well as within the structure of the church.

Probably the first thing we think of is the Great Commission. In Matthew 28:19,20 (King James Version) Jesus' last words to His disciples before returning to the Father were, "Go ye into all the world and preach the gospel to all people, baptizing them in the name of the Father, and the Son, and the Holy Ghost, teaching them to observe all things whatsoever I have commanded you. And lo, I am with you always, even unto the end of the age." These words reflect our Savior's highest priority assignment for all His disciples, for this is the only way that God is truly glorified. Only as He is allowed to invade the hearts of humankind and burn out the dross of sin and replace it with Himself can He be lifted up. This is the pinnacle purpose of all of God's dealings with mankind.

There are no exceptions stated here. All Jesus' disciples are expected to take part in this essential assignment. However, the varied parts that believers play in the sharing of the gospel are truly limitless. "Faith cometh by hearing and hearing by the Word of God "[66] so the gospel needs to be shared through words spoken and written and broadcast so that people can receive the "gospel truth". Preaching, teaching, evangelism, witnessing, written literature, the media, the internet are all means of spreading the gospel. Any part we can play in these arenas, whether it be direct involvement, financial support, or prayer contributes to fulfillment of this Great Commission.

The universal church, all believers, is God's primary plan for the sharing of the gospel, as groups of believers band together in local churches to edify one another in order to contribute to the evangelistic imperative. God gives all believers gifts to be invested through their individual lives as well as through the local church in His evangelistic efforts both locally and worldwide.[67] It hallows our sometimes seemingly insignificant church service to realize that we are joining hands with fellow believers worldwide and with our

God in fulfilling His greatest passion on earth. We need to never lose sight of the glory, privilege, and responsibility of the calling to ministry through our local church. Whatever we do that builds up and strengthens God's believers and/or God's church ultimately furthers God's evangelistic efforts both locally and worldwide. As believers and the church are strong and vital, God's outreach to the unsaved will flourish.

However, we should not see our contribution to evangelism as just what we do through our local church. Many para-church ministries manned by believers are making powerful impact on the needs of special groups of individuals, and through that influence bringing Christ's love to these people. Crisis pregnancy centers, helping ministries to needy and homeless, international relief organizations. prison ministries, etc. are all places where God wants to use His children to touch needy people with His love and sufficiency.

Additionally, "lifestyle evangelism" has become a popular concept for sharing the gospel. As we live out our faith through a lifestyle of righteous living and caring concern, our authenticity will build trust relationships wherein we can witness to the gospel we believe. Taking homemade soup to a neighbor who has just come home from the hospital; babysitting for a single Mom so she can have a night out; sending a card to a sick co-worker; relating to unsaved, ungodly family members unconditionally and non-judgmentally; helping someone in a crisis, etc. We need to approach every relationship-family, neighborhood, workplace, church, social, recreational-committed to loving unconditionally so that we can create influence in peoples' lives through which God may be able to work. Then these gestures of love will reflect God's love and create a thirst for more of Him. Jesus' kindness and compassion shown to the Samaritan woman at the well[168] perfectly illustrates lifestyle evangelism. After He showed concern for her personally, He was able to transition into a discussion of her spiritual need. Lifestyle evangelism is a very effective means of fulfilling the Great Commission. A classic book on the subject is Paul E. Little's How To Give Away Your Faith.[69]

Some believers think that if they just live a good life they are doing enough. I don't think so. Millions of people live a good life, but it has nothing to do with God, He does not get the glory, and people are not brought into His Kingdom. For God to get the glory we have to tie in the "light" that people see in our lives with the source of that light, Jesus Christ. We don't have to be highly articulate; God can use our simple efforts as He empowers them through His Spirit. Just ask Moses. We do need to "...be prepared to give a reason for the hope that is in us."[70] Writing out our testimony. Memorizing Scripture. Practicing sharing a presentation of the gospel. If we are committed to obedience to His Commission, do this kind of preparation, and believe in the God-man cooperative in us, God will provide us with opportunities and He will witness to Himself through us. That's a promise.

Another way in which usefulness to God is often described is in terms of warfare. God wants His children to be soldiers in the colossal, eternal battle between Himself and Satan, between good and evil. That description may sound a little extreme. Is everything in life really always a spiritual battle? I'm not radical about the concept of spiritual warfare. I don't see demons lurking behind every incident in life. But I absolutely believe that every moment of human existence is lived either for God or for Satan. Jesus said, "He who is not with me is against me, and he who does not gather with me scatters."[71] What is not good is therefore evil. At its most basic, every thought, feeling, motive, attitude and action is prompted either by love or by selfishness. God is love; Satan is selfishness. Love is holy; selfishness is sin and evil.

The story of spiritual warfare began in eternity past with Lucifer's rebellion and subsequent expulsion from heaven. With God's creation of humankind, His most cherished thing in all the universe, the warfare intensified, since God planned to fill His universe with holiness through this race created in His image. Satan's campaign against humankind started in the Garden of Eden as the snake seduced Adam and Eve to disobey God and sin entered the human race. The prophesy to Satan embodied in the serpent was that "He (Christ) will crush your head, and you will strike His heel."[72] The battle was engaged! Throughout Old Testament history Satan's attempts to sabotage the Hebrew race through whom the Messiah was promised are documented.

When Jesus appeared in human history, grew into manhood and began His earthly ministry, full-scale hostilities between He and Satan intensified mightily. Throughout the gospel accounts of Jesus' life the battle between good and evil is described. He cast out demons; He wrestled with Satan 40 days in the desert, as Satan tempted Him to sin; through His healing miracles He overcame (temporarily) the impact of sin's presence in human flesh; He confronted evil wherever He saw it, even in the Pharisees' hypocritical religiosity. And on the most evil day in human history, the world went dark and the heavens were shaken as the most violent conflagration of all time was waged on a hill called Golgotha. Love irrevocably triumphed over evil as Jesus died for the sin of all mankind and uttered those victorious words, "It is finished!" When Jesus arose from the tomb after defeating sin, death, and hell itself, He made it possible for human beings to experience that same victory. Though Satan was eternally defeated at that moment, He did not slink away in shame but continues to mercilessly pound away at men and women who are standing at the battlefront, fighting spiritual battles as part of God's army. Though the war is lost, Satan will continue His spiritual campaign against mankind until he is finally put into the lake that burns with fire forever[73].

The story of Job's experiences described in the Old Testament book of the same name is perhaps the most unmistakable illustration of God's intent to use our lives to fight spiritual battles. Job experienced a sequence of intensely painful events unparalleled in human history. This despite God's description of him to Satan as "...my servant Job... no one on earth is like him; he is blameless and upright, a man who fears God and shuns evil."[74] Several paramount life lessons can be learned from Job's experience. As already discussed previously, being a "good Christian" does not protect us from intense pain and loss. God's spiritual, eternal purposes are beyond our knowledge or understanding. As described in Job 1 and 2, sometimes unbeknownst to us there are spiritual battles being waged between God and Satan, and our lives are the battlefield. As God allowed Satan to test Job through intense suffering, nevertheless Scripture says, "In all this, Job did not sin..."[75] God wants our lives to showcase the greater power of His good over Satan's' evil. We may never know of these battles until we get to heaven, but the book of Job demonstrates that they do exist.

In Ephesians 6 we are instructed "Put on the full armor of God so that you can take your stand against the devil's schemes. For our struggle is not against flesh and blood, but against the rulers, against the authorities, against the powers of this dark world and against the spiritual forces of evil in the heavenly realms."[76] The armor described here is the belt of truth, the breastplate of righteousness, the gospel of peace, the shield of faith, the helmet of salvation, and the sword of the Spirit which is the Word of God. Having prepared ourselves for war by putting on these implements of battle we are fit soldiers, ready to be mightily used by God in His defense of His holy purposes in the battles fought where our lives are lived.

We may not see overt evidence of spiritual warfare "where our lives are lived". In our "civilized", sophisticated world talking about spiritual warfare may sound bizarre and extreme. But the Bible makes it clear it is reality. 1 Peter 5:8 says, "your enemy the devil prowls around like a roaring lion looking for someone to devour." A roaring lion is not very civilized; when he roars it's too late to defend yourself. He's already stealthily crept up on you and he knows he's got you. Unless we recognize his destructive intentions against us and vigilantly defend ourselves, he will devour us. So it is with Satan. We need to consciously make use of every part of our spiritual armor to fight the holy battle of good versus evil.

The temptation to do evil abounds in the world in which we live. Most of us recognize the temptation to commit obvious, overt forms of sin. Probably Satan is most successful in starting small in his attempts to destroy us. One "little sin" leads to another sin and another sin until "suddenly" we commit adultery, or lie outrageously, or hate, or wound our partner, or cheat...the list could go on forever.

A recent experience I had practically illustrates this point. I became irritated at my husband because he was not giving me the attention I wanted (a common complaint of wives about husbands, I might note). I hostilely withdrew from him, intending to "punish him" by giving him the cold shoulder. But instead I went into the bedroom and sat down in the bent-wood rocker where I have my daily devotions, and began to talk to God about what I was feeling. I asked myself, "In what way am I glorifying God with this behavior? I thought about the description of love in 1 Corinthians 13:4-8. "Love is patient, love is kind. It does not envy, it does not boast, it is not proud. It is not rude, it is not self-seeking, it is not easily angered, it keeps no record of wrongs. Love does not delight in evil but rejoices with the truth. It always protects, always trusts, always hopes, always perseveres. Love never fails..." I asked myself, "In what way am I practicing uncon-ditional love with this behavior?" The obvious answer was that I was being selfish and unloving, and not glorifying or obeying God.

I made a decision that the right thing to do was to return to my husband's side and be loving, and at an appropriate time talk to him about my feelings. What a battle ensued with that decision! It felt like my insides were on fire. I felt intense resistance to following this decision. I felt hot rage. But I persevered by prayer for God's help, and eventually was able to rejoin my husband. We had a wonderful morning, having devotions and praying together and later talking about how I had felt. It became a beneficial experience in our walk of love together. Had I not resisted Satan and his temptation to be unloving, our day would have gone his way rather than God's. This "small sin" could have led to increasingly more serious hurtful acts by myself and my husband which ultimately could have done great damage to our marriage.

Most often Satan's great victories start with "small sins." Through these subtle victories he creeps closer and closer to the moment of his final, roaring attack when he destructively eats us alive. Be alert. Use the full armor of God. "Resist the Devil and he will flee from you."[77]

As discussed in the previous chapter, God uses suffering as part of His process of changing and maturing us. This is preparation for another significant way that God wants to use us: to recycle His love and comfort that we've experienced into the lives of others who suffer as we have suffered. 2 Corinthians 1:4-6 says, "Who comforts us in all our troubles, so that we can comfort those in any trouble with the comfort we ourselves have received from God. For just as the sufferings of Christ flow over into our lives, so also through Christ our comfort overflows. If we are distressed, it is for your comfort and salvation; if we are comforted, it is for your comfort, which produces in you patient endurance of the same sufferings we suffer." God allows suffering, among other reasons, to make us compassionate reservoirs of His tenderness and comfort and help, so that we are ready to touch the lives of others with the same comfort which He gave to us.

A client I dealt with a few years ago had been embezzling money from his company and, under conviction from God, had turned himself in to his employers and legal authorities. We worked together to unravel the addictive gambling pattern that had dominated his life. Eventually he experienced healing and freedom from the power of the addiction. Providential circumstances led him to an organization that ministered to gambling addicts and he became a volunteer there. He has since been used by God to impact many person's lives, not only helping them overcome gambling addiction but also helping them put Christ on the throne of their lives. A marvelous illustration of the powerful truth that there is no such thing as wasted pain in HopeFound.

"Act Three: Being Used by God" can play out in many different ways in our lives in HopeFound. It can be godly love and character being used by God for His often unknown purposes; it can be participation in the evangelistic effort through many different means, both through church, parachurch and missions involvement, and individual witness; it can be fighting the good fight against Satan and evil; it can be recycling God's healing touch into others' lives. However our usefulness to God plays out, could it be reduced to its core, essential characteristic it would be love. All God's many characteristics can be summarized as facets of love. So also with us as He changes us into His image. Love, defined as doing what benefits others even at sacrifice to oneself, could be used synonymously for holiness. Holiness could be defined as love in action. Love and holiness could both be defined as absolute goodness, or absolute "Godness".

Every way in which God wants to use us, every purpose described in the Word, ultimately leads to the production of pure holy love. Evangelism leads to souls being saved who become more like God and impart His holy love to their world... teaching of believers leads to edification of the church which leads to evangelism which leads to souls being saved who become more like God and impart His holy love to their world...loving my family leads to spiritual influence which leads to souls being saved who become more like God and impart His holy love to their world...lifestyle evangelism leads to souls being saved who become more like God and impart His holy love to their world... overcoming Satan in the battle of good versus evil leads to spiritual victory which yields personal spiritual strength which God can use for evangelistic influence which leads to souls being saved who become more like God and impart His holy love to their world...comforting someone who is suffering with the comfort God has given me leads to their being spiritually strengthened to continue their work in God's Kingdom which leads to evangelistic opportunities which leads to people beings saved who become more like God and impart His holy love to their world. Is the pattern becoming obvious here? The Great Commission and the command to love thy neighbor and thy God are the same. Each supports the other; each produces the other. And the ultimate outcome is that God's holy love is magnified throughout the universe.

The greatest calling of life and the only one that really matters is the call to be used by God. His desire is that this would be a constant in our lives, occurring throughout all of the moments of life as we yield ourselves totally to His Spirit for His intentions, known and unknown. Whatever form God's using of us takes, it is always for one ultimate purpose, the increase of His Kingdom as His pure, holy love is reproduced through us and then in those whose lives we touch. God's bottom line is always holiness and love.

Notes
[58] Philippians 1:20,21
[59] Genesis 1:27
[60] Ephesians 2:10
[61] Psalms 139:16
[62] Jeremiah 1:5
[63] Ephesians 4:11,12

[64] 1 Corinthians 10:31
[65] 1 Corinthians 3:12
[66] Romans 10:17
[67] 1 Corinthians 12:29-31
[68] John 4:4-26
[69] Little, Paul E., <u>How To Give Away Your Faith</u>.
[70] 1 Peter 3:15, KJV
[71] Matthew 12:30
[72] Genesis 3:15
[73] Revelations 20:10
[74] Job 1:8
[75] Job 1:22; 2:10
[76] Ephesians 6:11,12
[77] James 4:7

For Personal Reflection:

1. Consider the concept of you and God in partnership, a "God-man cooperative," to accomplish His specific purposes planned just for you before time began. How have you experienced this before in your life? In what ways are you experiencing it today? If you are not, what do you need to do to begin to live out the God-man cooperative?

2. In your daily life are you consciously aware every moment of the potential of your being used by God? Are there areas of your life that you exclude from availability to God for His purposes?

3. In what way do you see yourself fulfilling the "evangelistic imperative," e.g., local church involvement, para-church ministry, lifestyle evangelism, financial support ?" Write up a personal

testimony incorporating the gospel and share it with someone.

4. Are you wearing the "full armor of God" or has Satan disabled you as a warrior in the spiritual battle of good vs. evil?

5. Thinking of God's wonderful promise in 2 Corinthians that He will enable us to comfort others with the same comfort that He has given us, have you experienced being used by God in that way? Is there some way that you can comfort someone today?

6. Does the love of God shine out of your life in ways that glorify God and bless others?

WHEN THE
CURTAIN COMES DOWN

The last chapter in the drama of our lives will be played out in heaven for eternity. At God's appointed time we will exit off the stage of our lives in HopeFound and arrive in the marvelous place which Jesus has been preparing for us every since he returned to heaven.[78] I don't intend to write a theological discussion of prophesies regarding the end-times. The nature of this book does not require it. But here is what Revelations has to say about our future eternal dwelling place:

"Then I saw a new heaven and a new earth, for the first heaven and the first earth had passed away, and there was no longer any sea. I saw the Holy City, the new Jerusalem, coming down out of heaven from God, prepared as a bride, beautifully dressed for her husband. And I heard a loud voice from the throne saying, 'Now the dwelling of God is with men, and he will live with them. They will be His people, and God himself will be with them and be their God. He will wipe every tear from their eyes. there will be no more death or mourning or crying or pain, for the old order of things has passed away... And he carried me away in the Spirit to a mountain great and high, and showed me the Holy City, Jerusalem, coming down out of heaven from God. It shone with the glory of God, and its brilliance was like that of a very precious jewel, like a jasper, clear as crystal. It had a great, high wall with twelve gates, and with twelve angels at the gates. On the gates were written the names of the twelve tribes of Israel. There were three gates on the east, three on the north, three on the south and three on the west. The wall of the city had twelve foundations, and on them were the names of the twelve apostles of the Lamb...The wall was made of jasper, and the city of pure gold, as pure as glass. The foundations of the city walls were decorated with every kind of precious stone. The first foundation was jasper, the second sapphire, the third chalcedony, the fourth emerald, the fifth sardonyx, the sixth carnelian, the seventh chrysolite, the eighth beryl, the ninth topaz, the tenth chrysoprase, the eleventh jacinth, and the twelfth amethyst. The twelve gates were twelve pearls, each gate made of a single pearl. The great street of the city was of pure gold, like transparent glass.

> I did not see a temple in the city, because the Lord God Almighty and the Lamb are its temple. The city does not need the sun or the moon to shine on it, for the glory of God gives it light, and the Lamb is its lamp. The nations will walk by its light, and the kings of the earth will bring their splendor into it. On no day will its gates ever be shut, for there will be no night there. The glory and honor of the nations will be brought into it. Nothing impure will ever enter it, nor will anyone who does what is shameful or deceitful, but only those whose names are written in the Lamb's book of life.

> Then the angel showed me the river of the water of life, as clear as crystal, flowing from the throne of God and of the Lamb down the middle of the great street of the city. On each

side of the river stood the tree of life, bearing twelve crops of fruit, yielding its fruit every month. And the leaves of the tree are for the healing of the nations. No longer will there be any curse. The throne of God and of the Lamb will be in the city, and his servants will serve him. They will see his face, and his name will be on their foreheads. There will be no more night. They will not need the light of a lamp or the light of the sun, for the Lord God will give them light. And they will reign forever and ever."[79]

it is intensely exciting to read these words and try to imagine what heaven will be like! To know that the Godhead will make their dwelling place with us-we will eternally be in their presence! We will dwell in a place beautiful beyond compare. Think of the beauty of an awesome sunset, or magnificent mountain view, or a sweet infant's precious face. Extreme beauty gives pleasure. For eternity we will experience beauty so total it will give acute, intense pleasure continually, beauty that shines with the glory of God. There will be no night, but a constant, beautiful light emanating throughout heaven: the light of the presence of God.

There will be no more death or mourning or crying or pain! Paradise Lost will be no more! It is thrilling to know that we will no longer be burdened with the physical, emotional, and spiritual struggles of living in our sinful flesh. There will be no sin in heaven! The battles will be over! Instead we will bask in the glorious, divine light of God's presence and worship and serve Him for all eternity.

The most thrilling thing about heaven for me will be seeing Jesus face to face "...They will see His face...". Several Bible verses[80] tell about crowns that we can earn through faithfulness, perseverance and service during our spiritual journey on planet earth. In heaven true justice will finally be experienced as our faithfulness through all the circumstances and seasons of life is recognized by our God. Our cooperation with God in seeking first His kingdom in the midst of all the joy and pain of Paradise Lost will finally be rewarded. Paul said in Roman 8:18 that our present sufferings are not worth comparing with the glory that will be revealed in us. These crowns will reflect glory to God through all eternity and make all the struggles of Paradise Lost nothing by comparison. I am absolutely committed to faithful service. I look forward eagerly to laying those crowns at Jesus' feet and them honoring Him throughout eternity. That will be eternal joy!

In Matthews 25 Jesus told the parable of the master who went away and entrusted his servants to profitably invest the talents He gave to them while he was gone. Upon His return those servants who had been faithful in the use of their talents heard the words, "Well done, thou good and faithful servant...".[81] The supreme motivator in my life is to envision that incredible day when I lay my crowns at His feet and hear those stirring words of appreciation! I believe the sound of those words spoken by our beloved Savior will echo throughout the eons of eternity and continually give intense pleasure, reminding us that we have pleased and honored Him.

I can only try to imagine what we will do forever and forever and forever...The Bible says that we *cannot* imagine the things that God has prepared for us.[82] I believe that, since God does not change, He will still be infinitely creative, and that creativity will be focused on continuously expanding His transcendent goodness in magnificent ways. I believe we will continue to participate in a God-man cooperative with him in this wondrous endeavor. However, our participation with God in His marvelous eternal pursuits will be unencumbered by any of the weaknesses of sinful human flesh. We will have a perfected body[83] and be able to do all the things that Jesus did after His resurrection. Makes the "sci fi" thrillers pale in comparison!

A final thought about heaven. It will be perfect! Paradise will be restored! We will have perfect knowledge and perfect love. 1 Corinthians 13:8-13 says, "Love never fails. But where there are prophecies they will cease; where there are tongues, they will be stilled; where there is knowledge, it will pass away. For we know in part and we prophesy in part, but when *perfection* comes, the imperfect disappears. When I was a child, I reasoned like a child. When I became a man, I put childish ways behind me. Now we see but a poor reflection as in a mirror; then we shall see face to face. Now I know in part; then I shall know fully, even as I am fully known. And now these three remain: faith, hope and love. But the greatest of these is love." Heaven will be perfect because love will be absolute. God - love - holiness - perfection. These are all inseparably woven together. Each is synonymous with the other. Each is a necessary distinctive of the other. Each co-exists with the other, God being the source of all. Since God is perfect love and will be everywhere present in heaven, and He will impart that perfect love to us, every moment of our eternal existence in heaven will be permeated with perfect, divine love.

Let's just think about that for a moment. I recently spent the weekend with members of our family with whom we have a wonderfully loving relationship. The moment they arrived, my heart was filled with the sweet, delicious feeling of simply adoring these people. It was so precious it almost hurt. They reciprocated to us the same loving response. Heaven will be like that, only better! Human love cannot compare with the divine love of heaven. With God, Jesus, the Holy Spirit, and with every other inhabitant of heaven, this most delightful of all human experiences will happen continuously forever!

Though we are limited in our human finite minds to comprehend fully what heaven will be like, this is what we do know: in the presence of God, Jesus, and the Holy Spirit continuously; dwelling in a place beautiful beyond compare; experiencing the joy of Jesus' pleasure with us eternally; participating in marvelous, colossal endeavors with God; complete freedom from sin and suffering; perfect knowledge and perfect love in a perfect place with our perfect God. Paradise restored!! Though Satan for a season interfered with God's highest desire for us, in heaven all will be made perfect again for all eternity. No wonder Paul said he groaned, longing to be clothed with his heavenly dwelling,[84] and in another place he said that to die would be gain and that he desired to depart and be with Christ, which is far better.[85] Heaven will be worth it all!

The Revelation passage referenced above says that "only those whose names are written in the Lamb's Book of Life" will be in heaven. That phrase, "Book of Life", is used several other times in Scripture, in both the Old and New Testament, to refer to a divine registry of those who are citizens of God's community. Perhaps the most vital question of all time that each of us needs to ask himself is "Is my name written in the Lamb's Book of Life?" Because I have become a child of God through faith in Jesus Christ, my name has been entered on that decisive list of those who will enjoy eternal life in heaven! I can't wait to go there! In the mean time, like Paul, "Forgetting what is behind and straining toward what is ahead, I press on toward the goal to win the prize for which God has called me heavenward in Christ Jesus."[86]

Notes
[78] John 14:2,3
[79] Revelations 21:1-4, 10-14, 18-27; 22:1-5
[80] 1 Corinthians 9:25, 11 Timothy 4:8, James 1:12, 1 Peter 5:4, Revelations 2:10

[81] Matthew 25:21
[82] 1 Corinthians 2:9
[83] Philippians 3:21
[84] 11 Corinthians 5:1,2
[85] Philippians 1:22,23
[86] Philippians 3:13,14

For Personal Reflection...

1. Get away with God to a quiet place, and thought-fully read and meditate on the verses describing heaven. With eyes closed, visualize life in heaven as best you can. Include in that vision yourself laying at Jesus' feet the crowns you have earned for faithful service, and hearing "Well done, good and faithful servant..."

2. Read Philippians 1:21 and 3:13 and 14, Romans 8:18, 1 John 3:3, and Matthew 6:33. Prayerfully and with conviction write your personal response to these truths about heaven, as illustrated in these scriptures. Make this response a part of your daily time of prayer with God.

3. Ask yourself if you have any doubts about your name being written in the Book of Life. Be honest. If you have doubts, seek help from a pastor or wise Christian friend to settle this most important issue.

HOPEFOUND: PURSUING A NEW LIFESTYLE

One of my all-time heroes is Mother Teresa. I always marveled at her selfless life of ministry to the down-trodden of society. She lived her entire adult life with no material goods whatsoever. What was her secret that allowed her to live with serenity and peace, without the stuff that most of the rest of human kind spend a lifetime seeking? To quote Mother Teresa (from several sources in the public domain):

> "we are at Jesus' disposal. If he wants you to be sick in bed, if He wants you to proclaim His word in the street, that's all right, *every-thing is all right. We   must say, 'I belong to you. You can do whatever you like...* What is poverty? Poverty is freedom. It is freedom so that *what I possess doesn't own me, so that what I possess doesn't hold me down, so that my possessions don't keep me from sharing or giving of myself...* He could put me here. He could put me there. He can use me. He can

*not use me. It doesn't matter, because I belong
so totally to Him that He can do just what He
wants to do with me...* Be at Christ's disposal to
such a degree that Christ can make use of you
without having to ask, 'May I? Can't I? Will
you allow me?' *It is something very beautiful
and freeing to be able to give ourselves fully
to Jesus, each in our own way."*

She had discovered life in HopeFound. She had crossed
that river into the sanctuary of intimate, personal communion
with God that freed her soul from pursuit of the world's goods
to joyful investment of her whole being in doing good. She was
probably one of the most joyful, humble people of the twentieth century; she was also one of the most influential. When
she spoke, it made the headlines. Her strong condemnation
of the United States for the wholesale abortion of her babies
became a classic quote repeated over and over in numerous
media. Because she yielded to God and allowed Him to do His
will in and through her life, He made her a person of tremendous spiritual and social influence and impact. Only eternity
will reveal the myriad ways in which she touched her world
with sacred significance.

During my journey through the "dark season of my
soul" God brought a remarkable book into my path called
Descending into Greatness,[87] by Bill Hybels. In this book Mr.
Hybels elaborates on the Scripture passage in Philippians 2:5-
11. The message of the book is that Christ set the example
of descending into greatness: he left heaven for this planet to
serve and save humanity, and in that descent accomplished
the greatest thing ever done in human history. As His children
we are likewise to follow His example of sacrificing our lives
in service of love to those He brings our way. To quote Mr.
Hybels:

"God is calling on Christians to develop the discipline of losing. *If you want to follow me,* God says, *follow the example of My Son, who lost not just a little, or even a lot, but lost everything...* God's call to lose for His sake doesn't mean we deny the legitimate needs of our human frame or the desires and passions He has placed within us... But losing does mean that we allow God to determine what needs are legitimate. Losing means to yield our desires and passions to His guidance; to invite Him to chip away the rough edges of our personalities; to use our gifts without seeking applause; and to allow Him to conform our dreams to His will...

Yet God asks us to lose so we can gain. He makes a hard request then makes a promise. *Lose your selfish ambition; I will honor you for loving others. Lose your addiction to things; I will provide for you if you seek me wholeheartedly. Lose your obsession to be in control; I will give you power as you follow Me. Lose your appetite for thrills; I will startle you with pleasures you could never have found on your own. Lose your life; I will give you eternity.*

It is a seemingly brutal path love often takes; a life of losing, of self-demotion, even dying. But the Bible is stubbornly insistent about this: it is, at the same time, the path that leads to joy." [88]

Interspersed throughout <u>Descending Into Greatness</u> are stories of real twentieth century people whose lives exemplify the selfless, servant heart of our savior. One such person is Lance Murdock, a trader on the Chicago Board of Trade who, before becoming a Christian, allowed his consuming need to succeed to bring about terrible financial disaster.

> "Slowly Lance Murdock came to the realization that the real disaster in his life was not losing nearly $1.4 million, it was the bankruptcy of his thinking. It was the belief that he could build for himself an indestructible world, an environment where nothing could get through-failure, fear, the thief in the middle of the night. If he could stack circumstances-his bank account, his trading reputation, his successes-then he could always count his own self-worth. The plan backfired... 'I realized that I placed my value and importance as a human being on superficial successes,"[89] Mr. Murdock said.

Mr. Hybels describes the change in Murdock after realigning his life with God's purposes:

> "He has changed his focus as a trader... He feels an intense responsibility to represent Christ. Many of the traders have noticed the difference in his demeanor... He knows that he has a rare opportunity to bring the gospel to people mostly absorbed in self-promotion."[90]

Mr. Murdock's "descent into greatness" did not involve an external change in his life circumstances. It was an internal change in what he was now living for. Other individuals in the book did remarkably change their life circumstances to "descend into greatness", such as Dr. Jim Judge, who left a lucrative medical practice in West Chicago to minister to the poorest of the poor in Kenya, South Africa.

<u>Descending Into Greatness</u> is about Hope Found in Paradise Lost. It was one of a number of significant tools used by God to hone the metaphor in my needy, hope-seeking heart. It describes the dramatically changed lifestyle which the metaphor challenges us to live out in HopeFound, one of demoting our pursuit of comfort and safety for the greater pursuit of God's higher purposes in our lives As with the individuals used as illustrations in the book, relocating to HopeFound sometimes does not require any change in the circumstances of a life, just a relocation of God's priorities to the throne of my heart. Sometimes that relocation to HopeFound demands the sacrifice of everything heretofore important in life.

Most Christians are familiar with the story of Joni Erickson Tada. Following a diving accident at age 18 that left her a quadriplegic, Joni begged God to die, and feverishly sought how she might commit suicide. Her wall of protection had failed her beyond miserably, and she did not want to live on this hellish planet. Her book, <u>Joni</u>,[91] chronicles her journey from deep depression and despair to a life of great achievement for God's Kingdom, personal satisfaction, and joy. She heads a remarkable ministry to disabled people around the world, sings and paints professionally, has a world-wide speaking and writing ministry, and is married to a devoted husband, Ken Tada. Thank God that before she could figure out how a quadriplegic could commit suicide, He had wooed her lovingly and gently yet firmly to relocate to HopeFound. She accepted her circumstances (over which she had no control anyway), allowing them to become very effective props on the stage of her life, turned her life over to God to do with as He would, and He has done miraculous things. She "descended into greatness" as she made HopeFound her permanent earthly residence.

I have a very close personal friend who is my "up close and personal" hero. She has had unspeakable suffering in her personal life: an abusive former husband, children whose lives reflect the dysfunction that living with abuse can do to a soul; a grandchild born with hideous birth defects who died after several years of intense suffering. Yet Nancy* reflects a serene, warm, servant spirit which blesses everyone fortunate enough to get close to her. Often I am amazed at her ability to remain unruffled, steadfast, and focused on her many ministries, when I know what she is dealing with moment-by-moment in her life. She teaches Sunday School, leads an in-home adult Bible study, sings, writes poetry, paints, speaks, and always warms peoples' hearts with her caring ways. Nancy* learned the lesson long ago that chasing after elusive dreams is a thankless, consuming task. She dreams different dreams now; dreams that have God's marvelous plans for her life at the center of her being.

I am not suggesting that life in HopeFound is always miserable and unfulfilling personally, and the only joy we experience is the joy of spiritual ministry and accomplishment. Good things do happen to God's people. Sometimes God's sovereignty includes props on the stage of life in HopeFound that are delightful and full of pleasure and ease, and meet dreams and desires of our hearts. Unique to life in HopeFound, however, is the attitude that everything that appears on the stage of life, whether bitter or sweet, be willingly accepted as providentially there for God's intended spiritual good, and that good be pursued above all else. A hand held out open to God, with all I possess available for His sovereign purposes, is a prerequisite to residence in HopeFound.

Whatever the season of life, whatever the circumstances, approaching them with a HopeFound perspective will enable us to live out God's intentions for our lives with purpose, power, and peacefulness. Whether it be in our marriage relationship, our role as parents, our friendships, workplace relationships, our ministry, dealing with suffering or loss, etc., the principles of HopeFound living give freedom, joy, focus, peace, and powerful impact.

PRINCIPLES OF HOPEFOUND LIVING

Let's define the basic principles of HopeFound living portrayed in the metaphor:

1. Accept that, because we live in Paradise Lost, life will have its share of disappointment, injustice, loss, and suffering.
2. Give up the self-absorbed pursuit of circumstantial comfort, of pain-free living, as the ultimate purpose of life.
3. Embrace absolute devotion to God and His spiritual, eternal purposes as life's highest calling.
4. Seek continuing spiritual growth and vigor through Bible study and prayer and through pursuit of a renewed mind that thinks God's thoughts in all circumstances.
4. View all life circumstances as allowed by God and intended for   knowing Him better, growing spiritually, and being used by Him, in order that His love and goodness be shared with our world.
5. Trust God's good purposes in all circumstances, even painful, and always actively seek to fulfill His eternal, spiritual intentions.
6. Remember and find hope in the eternal heaven awaiting us, where all will finally be made perfect.

Marriage is perhaps the toughest place to practice HopeFound living. More than any other circumstance in life we elevate marriage to the impossible position of being the source of perfect needs fulfillment, and we often make the unspoken, futile demand that our partner meet all the needs of our heart. Every soul-wound we carry insists that finally in our marriage we will find relief and healing. We want our married life to be Ozzie and Harriet perfect. We won't allow for any imperfection in this corner of our Paradise Lost world. Thus marriage often becomes a chronic, joy-killing power struggle between two people each determined their partner will be the perfect mate they want them to be.

We need to correct the unrealistic expectations we place on our marriages. In metaphorical language, we need to see that our marriage, like every other circumstance in life, is not a major plank in a wall of protection, but is a prop on the stage of our life through which God intends to work His good purposes in us and through us. We need to take our self-centered needs-fulfillment off the throne of our heart and instead make our goal be fulfilling God's purposes through the struggles of our marriage. Marriage challenges us to grow like no other experience in life. Getting our focus on the growth God wants to see in us instead of on our unmet needs will free us to pursue a lifestyle of unconditional love. Accepting the inevitability of imperfections in our partners and viewing those challenges as opportunities for personal growth, we can choose to respond to them with blessing rather than retaliation.

Practicing unconditional love, or *agape* love, is an incredibly challenging discipline requiring extraordinary wisdom and perseverance. It means that I do not condition my treatment of you on your treatment of me or your worthiness of my love. I choose to act in ways that benefit you, not because of who you are but because of who I am in Christ, because of His love created by God's Spirit in me. Only through supernatural, Holy Spirit power can we self-centered human beings exercise unconditional love. How else can we obey the command to love our enemies?

Unconditional love is not permission for mistreatment and abuse. We can set boundaries and confront wrong respectfully, while still demonstrating love throughout the moments of our lives together.

> You could cut the tension in the room with a knife the first day I met Steve* and Jenny*. They sat stone-faced and silent in the reception area, cold, hopeless, despair etched on both their faces. Physically attractive and materially prosperous,, it was hard to understand how they could be so miserable.
>
> Steve was a very successful business owner who thrived on the challenges and admiration he achieved through his business success. He worked long hours, and on days off curried favor with clients by spending the day on the golf course with them. He expected Jenny to cook, clean, do laundry, run errands, take care of their infant daughter, organize his life for him, look beautiful at social events, be available sexually at his whim, and be really appreciative of the wonderful, affluent lifestyle all his hard work was providing for them.
>
> Jenny was furious. She saw Steve as absolutely self-centered, and felt used and devalued by him. Her needs seemed to be of no significance whatsoever to him. The world revolved around Steve. His treatment of her touched a deep soul-wound of neglect from her childhood with an alcoholic father and absent mother. As she had done then, she

coped with her pain in her marriage by hiding her feelings, trying to be super-woman and do everything Steve wanted of her. Until she just burned out.

Steve came to counseling for several sessions and then decided his work schedule did not permit him to be involved further. We had accomplished little in the brief time, and Jenny was willing to continue in counseling to work on "coping". After Jenny recognized the childhood soul-wound magnifying the pain of Steve's mistreatment of her, we saw this relationship as a God-given opportunity to address healing in those relationships from the past and then bring His healing into her marriage relationship. She accepted the challenge of seeking to live a lifestyle of unconditional love.

Recognizing that her boundaryless lifestyle, a pattern begun in her childhood, had encouraged Steve's narcissistic behavior, Jenny began setting healthier boundaries with his endless expectations of her, yet when he reacted in anger she continued to treat him in loving ways instead of withdrawing or counter-attacking, as she had done in the past. She told me this change was "the hardest thing she had ever done in her life." It required her to start everyday in prayer, seeking God's help at every moment.

Within a few months Jenny was reporting remarkable changes in Steve and wonderful changes in their relationship. Her unconditional love for him was challenging him to

> re-evaluate his treatment of her, and he was responding with consideration and respect.
> About six months later, Jenny called me to tell me they were expecting a baby, and happier than they had ever been.

When we take the spotlight off of our personal needs-fulfill-ment and place it instead on the fulfillment of God's purposes, the power of God is set free in our marriage relationship to bring positive change, not only in ourselves but in our part-ners as well. Unconditional love is the most powerful healing force in the universe. Living a lifestyle of unconditional love not only transforms us it also provides the fabulous bonus of transforming our partners. Viewing her marriage relationship as intended by God for her healing, growth, and service to Him, instead of pursuing self-centered fulfillment, ultimately gave Jenny the best marriage relationship possible.

Another very significant HopeFound perspective on marriage is that God's highest priority for our marriage, as we bond and become one in Him, is for our union to become a powerful, effective tool in His Kingdom work. God wants to use the synergy of our union to create an awesome parenting team, ministry team, witnessing team, prayer team, etc. If Satan can successfully keep us trapped in a self-absorbed power struggle with our partner, our marriage cannot be the potent tool in God's work He desires it to be. Better yet, if Satan can bring divorce out of the self-centered struggle, all God's wonderful intentions for our marriage will be subverted.

Parenting has its own unique challenges that require the HopeFound perspective. The biggest mistake parents make in this regard is to try to fulfill their needs rather than God's intentions through their childrens' lives. Metaphorically speaking our children can be unconsciously viewed as components useful for reinforcing our delusional wall of protection. Through their lives they will bring us self-worth, attention, love, security, praise, success, etc. Earlier I told about Carol, who attempted to use her role as parent to sustain her image of perfection. Anytime we as parents seek to meet our emotional needs through our children a role reversal of sorts has occurred which always interferes with our ability to provide the nurturing environment children need for healthy development.

Recently a mom brought her teenage son in for counseling, saying he had developed a rebellious, angry attitude. As we discussed their history, it became clear that he was rebelling against being expected to live out an identity not his own but one required by his Mom because of her history. She had grown up in a chaotic family where alcoholism and workaholism humiliated her and deprived her of the happy family life she yearned for. Marked by the soul-wounds of inferiority and abandonment, as a parent she was determined to win the self-worth she lacked through creating a family of extremely high-achievers. To protect herself from loneliness she controlled her family's lives through rigid expectations of family involvement and required "closeness". While his older sister had complied with his mother's requirements, this independent young man refused to be programmed to fulfill her needs.

Some parents draw their children into unhealthy alignments referred to as "emotional incest" by Dr. Pat Love in her book, The Emotional Incest Syndrome.[92]
They seek to draw emotional nurturance from their children and create a loyalty which binds the child to them even

long into adulthood, making it difficult for him/her to pursue normal adult relationships.

> Katy*, an eleven-year-old girl and an only child, struggled with compulsive behaviors and many anxiety symptoms when she came for counseling. Her Dad and Mom had a very fragile relationship, and had been separated several times. Both of them had sought to align with her against the other, sharing information with her she did not need to know, seeking her company and her approval. She could not really "have a life" because of her anxiety-driven need to somehow please both parents. What a "Catch 22" trap for a child!

Christian parents can fall into the trap of using their children to glorify their image as "super Christians." Sometimes Christian parents wrongly seek superiority and God's approval through rigid legalism, and expect their children to buttress that image through conforming to their unrealistic perceptions of godliness. They require their children to be in church every time the door is open and to fulfill every legalistic demand on the church's "list" without question in order to be acceptable.

> Dave, a seventeen year old high school senior, was ordered to counseling by his parents because they were ashamed of his behavior. He was dating a "wild," non-Christian girl, breaking curfew continually, skipping church, and even academically in trouble. He had always cooperated with the family lifestyle of intense involvement in their conservative church and its standards until recently. But as he approached adulthood and

his parents continued to rigidly control every
aspect of his life, requiring him to conform
to every nuance of their legalistic lifestyle in
order to maintain their status in the church,
his developing independence rebelled against
such forced conformity.

These are but a few examples of ways parents seek to
meet their needs through their children's lives, incorporating
their behavior and successes into their delusional walls of
protection. The changed perspective necessary for these
parents is to recognize their children as an awesome trust
from God who exist for His holy purposes and in whose
healthy emotional and spiritual development it is their privilege to invest. Our goal as parents should be to meet the
needs of our children in such a way that they enter adulthood
emotionally and spiritually healthy and ready to mature into
Godly adults.

A very distressing reality that parents really struggle to
accept is that we cannot protect our children from the pain
and suffering inevitable in Paradise Lost. We delusionally
extend our wall-building efforts to encompass them, and can
be shattered when we find those walls are not strong enough.
Like I did, loving parents try to provide the "perfect" environment of love, nurturance, discipline, physical protection,
spiritual guidance, educational opportunity, etc. for their
children, naively believing that their efforts have the power
to magically protect them from all harm. It can't be done in
Paradise Lost.

Distraught parents called to schedule a
conference session to discuss their teenage
daughter's recent suicide attempt. They told
of her spiraling disintegration in the last few
months into deep depression, self-mutila-

tion behavior, and then attempted suicide. Through counseling we ultimately discovered that their child had been molested by a baby-sitter for several years when she was very young, and recent dating experiences had triggered those memories. The intense grief these parents experienced in discovering this information came not only from their daughter's suffering but also from confronting the shocking truth that all their sincere efforts to provide a safe, secure childhood for their daughter had not been sufficient. They struggled with powerful feelings of anger, failure and guilt. Relief came as they accepted the limitations that we have in Paradise Lost to protect ourselves and the ones we love from the impact of sin's presence all around us, and claimed God's healing, redeeming love for their daughter's life.

As parents our goal needs to be to diligently provide the safest, healthiest environment we possibly can for our children. That is our responsibility, and in most cases that will be sufficient. But it is an unrealistic goal to expect to protect our children from all pain and suffering. There are no guarantees in Paradise Lost. Should suffering befall them, our spiritual and emotional survival and theirs depends on developing a HopeFound perspective that accepts the inevitable damage caused by sin's presence in Paradise Lost and our limited ability to protect them, and yet finds peace in trusting God's supreme power to heal and overcome sin's impact in their lives, both here and in heaven for eternity.

Disease, physical suffering, and death are yet other circumstances extremely difficult to handle which necessitate a HopeFound perspective. The question of why God allows suffering has been addressed in myriad sermons and books over the centuries. Reading one of these books would be wise for an in-depth discussion of this issue. Briefly, when we or someone we love suffers and even dies the typical human response, whether spoken or repressed, is to question and often blame God and feel rage at the injustice of it. He is too young; she was so good; he was so talented; she has suffered so much already; he was needed so badly by his family... The mind and emotions recycle endlessly through outraged thoughts and emotions, sometimes causing depression and/or physical illness.

When Vicki's* husband of over 20 years died after a lengthy struggle with cancer, she seemed to handle it well. Nevertheless, several years later she found herself on the verge of a nervous breakdown. Though she had a satisfying career, had been provided for well financially, and her teenage children were fine, responsible Christian young people, she was deeply depressed and found life meaningless and empty. Even getting up and going to work had become a major challenge.

As we revisited the long season of dealing with her husband's illness and death, gradually she unearthed deep feelings of outrage at the injustice of his suffering and his family's loss of his presence. Being a "good Christian" she had mouthed all the appropriate attitudes about his loss, and never given herself permission to feel what she truly felt, an essential for healthy grieving and closure. Her greatest sense of injustice came from the fact that they had been such a remarkably loving couple and family, far superior to most others, even

Christians. Why would God allow such a special family to be torn apart by loss? She felt that none of them would ever again feel the unique happiness they had previously experienced.

Additionally, they had prayed fervently for weeks, months, and years, yet it had made no difference. What about the promise that the prayer of a righteous man is powerful and effective?[93] What about the principle, "You do not have because you do not ask God?"[94] Where was the reap-what-you-sow reward for their Godly, faithful lifestyle?

Vicki* needed to develop a HopeFound perspective to finally resolve her grief over the loss of her husband. Like Vicki*, many of us have major misconceptions about suffering and death that need to be recognized and corrected. We need to accept the inevitability of suffering and death as part of life in Paradise Lost, and realize that no one is exempt from their touch, not even the "best Christian" (take a look at Job again...). Jesus said that rain falls on both the righteous and the unrighteous,[95] and Ecclesiastes[96] says there is a time to be born and a time to die, a time to weep and a time to laugh. We need to give up the delusion of a wall of protection ensuring a lifetime of happiness and fulfillment and allow God the sovereign right to choose the time of our and our family members' deaths, according to His righteous, good purposes.

Yielding to God's sovereignty even over the death of a loved one requires us to develop the trust in God's goodness to be able to say, like Job, "... though He slay me (or my husband, or my child), yet will I trust Him."[97] That kind of trust believes that God absolutely always works for the best SPIRITUAL good according to his omniscient wisdom, and that spiritual good is worth whatever pain and suffering God allows in our lives during our brief sojourn in Paradise Lost. We may not be able to comprehend with our limited, finite human mind how our or our loved one's suffering and/or death can be spiritually "good." But Isaiah 55:8 says, "For my thoughts are not your thoughts, neither are your ways my ways, declares the Lord. As the heavens are higher than the earth, so are my ways higher than your ways, and my thoughts than your thoughts." HopeFound trust believes absolutely in God's goodness and spiritually beneficial purposes in all life circumstances, whether those purposes are comprehensible to us or not. This perspective on suffering and death necessitates and forges a focus on the eternal future with God when all pain and loss will end and our faithfulness to Him will be eternally rewarded.

Therefore, in our prayers we will feel free to ask God for what we want, but submit our wants to God's infallible purposes without presuming to tell God what to do. In the Garden of Gethsemane Jesus said, "My Father, if it is possible, may this cup be taken from me. Yet not as I will but as you will."[98] His example demonstrated that we can be free to speak from the heart to God about our feelings, while at the same time remaining submissive to His sovereignty.

A final vital life issue to consider from a HopeFound perspective is that of **career and ministry**. Like every other life circumstance, these can be unconsciously perceived as planks in a wall of protection, pursued only to meet needs significant to my comfort and security, rather than viewed as props on the stage of my life through which the most important pursuit is the fulfillment of God's eternal purposes.

It may seem legitimate for the highest career goal of someone in a secular field to be success that "makes a living", that pays the bills and provides a comfortable life style. But from a HopeFound perspective it is not the highest priority, though it is vital. Rather our primary career goal as Christians needs to be to allow God to direct us to the work He planned for us, and as an employee or employer to live out the life of God in us in the workplace, allowing Him to prescribe the ethics, commitment, and personal traits we bring to our particular work situation. When there is a conflict between God's principles and the requirements for success in a career situation, God's principles have to come first.

Trusting God to meet our needs when our commitment to Godly principles may damage our career potential or even necessitate a job change is a challenging quandary. This is especially difficult for men who, through their lineage from Adam, were assigned by God the responsibility of providing for their families. Failing to meet their families' financial needs causes them deep feelings of anxiety and inadequacy. It may seem like a "Catch 22" conflict between two priorities, both given by God, when ethical issues at work press for taking a stand which may threaten our financial future. But embedded in that seeming dilemma is the tremendous growth opportunity to achieve a deeper level of trust in God than ever experienced before. We can test and prove that we can confidently live by God's principles no matter what, with no fear of the outcomes, because God's purposes and power are bigger than any difficult circumstance in life. If God allows a season of financial struggle, we can learn to rest in the conviction that He allows it only for the growth opportunity it presents for us, and in His promise that He will not allow His children who walk in obedience to Him to go without basic needs.[99]

Sometimes the dilemma people experience in their work situation is not a moral dilemma but a confusion of priorities. A pattern of over-commitment of time and energy to career, to the neglect of God, self, and family, is described as work-a-holism. It is an addiction driven by unconscious need to avoid emotional pain. The work-a-holic pursuit of career success can be fueled by an out-of-balance desire for the material goods that money can buy. The status that is accorded those who make money and can buy big houses, expensive cars, recreational vehicles, etc. is a soul-nourishing potion for those hampered by feelings of inadequacy and insignificance. "Success" itself can be the golden fruit sought obsessively as a means to overcome feelings of failure and inferiority. Likewise, accumulating lots and lots of money and the things it buys can be pursued to stave off the unconscious terror of returning to devastating poverty experienced in childhood.

In these situations, building walls of material success is unconsciously pursued as a way to protect from debilitating emotional pain. Though they may genuinely love God, the self-protective need to heal old wounds runs deeper even than their commitment to Him. That is what must change. Allowing anything to be more important to us than our availability to God is idol-worship, which God hates and is committed to abolish. He will engineer circumstances that challenge us to recognize and repent of worshipping the god of materialism and success, and free us from delusional wall-building to find our worth, significance, and security in Him and His Kingdom work.

Brad* came in for counseling reluctantly only after his wife insisted that he come or she would separate from him. She described constant family tension caused by Brad's work-a-holism and drinking. He was never available to his family as a positive presence, either because of his over-work or his aggressive hostility brought on by drinking.

Brad* was a millionaire who owned a highly successful business with several locations in the area. He drove an expensive sports car, dressed extremely well, gave money to many charities, and was an affable, likeable man. As he gradually became genuinely invested in the counseling process he shared more and more deeply about his childhood experiences of being orphaned and raised in extreme poverty by indifferent, distant relatives. Often he went to school dirty, hungry, and poorly clothed.

A breakthrough moment came when he sobbed that he had felt that there must be something really wrong with him to experience such shameful circumstances. He came to understand that both his drinking and his obsessive pursuit of business success were his way of protecting himself from ever feeling the shame and inferiority that living with abject poverty had inflicted on him. Even his charitable giving was tied in with the desire to alleviate the pain of poverty for others, a positive outcome from his own suffering.

As he developed a HopeFound perspective that recognized suffering as inevitable in Paradise Lost and not an indicator of shameful inferiority or God's disfavor, he came to believe in a God who valued and loved him even during his poverty-stricken childhood. He developed a healthy self-acceptance and desire to live according to God's priorities for himself and his family. Overcoming his problem drinking and overwork was a gradual but life-changing process which he ultimately accomplished.

Pursuit of career success can be a hidden but deeply entrenched pattern of delusional wall-building in Paradise Lost. If it interferes with God's higher priorities in our lives, we need to look deeper beneath the surface of our motives and discern what self-protective role it is unconsciously playing in our lives, and what changes we need to make to replace wall-building with God's sovereign purposes in our career situation. A HopeFound perspective sees career as about more than income or job satisfaction or fulfillment of emotional needs. Our career, like every other prop on the stage of our lives, is a place where God wants to accomplish His spiritual purposes in support of His Kingdom work.

An excellent illustration of this principle is R.J. LeTourneau. Struggling to keep a failing business venture afloat and not tithing, LeTourneau promised God that He would begin to tithe faithfully and wait on Him to bring success in his business. Gradually his business began to prosper, and gradually LeTourneau increased his tithe percentage from 10% to 20% to 30% ...until eventually he was tithing 90% of his business income. He also used his funds to establish a Christian engineering college, LeTourneau University in Texas. LeTourneau said his business became just a means to an end, that of making money to funnel into the Lord's work.

God's Kingdom purposes for our workplace may not be as grand as they were for LeTourneau. They may be something "up close and personal" such as challenging us to grow in the integrity and honesty we bring to our work situation, teaching us to seek first His Kingdom not material gain,[100] using our gracious, spirit-filled Godliness to minister to a co-worker, planting a seed of God's truth in a co-worker's heart and watering it faithfully, etc. HopeFound living always looks for God's greater intentions in all life circumstances and pursues them passionately.

Surprisingly, the same kind of hidden, self-protective motives can underlie Christian ministry as those described previously for secular careers. It may seem contradictory to suggest that someone in ministry could have self-centered motivation in their work. After all, the very word "ministry" derives from the root word "minister" which means to serve. In Christendom, ministry specifically refers to service that edifies and expands the body of Christ, the church universal. But as in secular careers, underlying our seemingly unselfish and even noble intentions in ministry can be a quest for the fulfillment of deep unmet emotional needs. Ministry achievement can unknowingly become a plank in a delusional wall of protection from emotional pain.

Let me state this disclaimer immediately: I am not suggesting that those in ministry careers are all striving for self-centered needs fulfillment. That is absolutely not the case. Most of those in ministry are there because they love God, are called by Him, and dedicated to serve Him, His purposes, and His church. They have the HopeFound perspective that every aspect of their ministry must be dedicated totally to God's plans and ways, and self-centered personal goals must not be allowed to subvert His intentions. God's work, to be of any eternal benefit, must be done from a heart with this Godly motivation.

But some in ministry have mixed motives and some are wolves in sheep's clothing. In the same way that secular careers can include efforts to meet needs for acceptance, worth, achievement, power, and security, Christian ministry can be undertaken for these same purposes. If a pastor preaches from a motive of success or approval, he probably does not preach God's message for his congregation. If a singer's song is for fame or achievement his popularity is his reward. If a missionary's zeal come from a burning desire to be "the best" and the mission is coincidental, the mission will abort. If a tele-evangelist preaches from a motive of power and financial gain, his ministry will ultimately fail spiritually if not organizationally. Recent history has demonstrated this point too well.

Additional benefits which can be sought, consciously or unconsciously, through Christian ministry, are the power and the automatic cloak of superiority awarded to "professional Christians," the (fictional) opportunity to earn extra points with God, or to do penance for previous sins, or to erase a profound sense of guilt inculcated by toxic parenting.

Christians in ministry are human and, just like everyone else, vulnerable to Satan's efforts to pollute their motives for their work with self-centered intentions. It would be absurd to suggest that everyone in Christian ministry must have absolutely pure motives at all times to be used by God. That is an impossible standard. Even if they are deeply devoted to God and sincerely submitting every part of their ministry to His direction and scrutiny, they will still not always have perfect motivation; after all, this is Paradise Lost. Yet God will use them mightily for the sincerity of their heart's passion to serve Him. Nevertheless, they have an awesome responsibility to be vigilant because they have been called to the greatest work on earth, the promotion of God's Kingdom. Of all the grievous sins that wall-building efforts can cause, the sin of sullying Christian service with self-centered motives does the most profound damage because it is eternal. To whatever degree Satan is successful in distracting those in Christian ministry from the unequivocal pursuit of God's purposes, he strikes a blow of eternal proportions.

I pray that reading this chapter, "Pursuing a HopeFound Lifestyle", has stirred up a deep thirst in you, the reader, to relocate to HopeFound. Can you sense the peace, the freedom from fear, the invigorating sense of purpose, the satisfaction of God-sanctioned achievement, the joy of God's approval everywhere present in this hallowed place? Do you yearn, as I did many years ago, for "hope found in Paradise lost"? If so, maybe it's time to cross the bridge.

Notes

[87] Hybels, Bill, <u>Descending Into Greatness</u>. Grand Rapids: Zondervan Publishing House.   1993
[88] Ibid., p. 21-22
[89] Ibid., p. 51
[90] Ibid., p. 54-55
[91] Eareckson Tada, Joni, <u>Joni</u>. Grand Rapids: Zondervan Publishing House. 1976, 1996
[92] Love, Dr. Patricia, <u>Emotional Incest Syndrome</u>. New York: Bantam Books. 1990
[93] James 5:16
[94] James 4:2
[95] Matthew 5:45
[96] Ecclesiastes 3:2,4
[97] Job 13:15 KJV
[98] Matthew 26:39
[99] Psalms 37:25
[100] Matthew 6:33

*fictitious name

For Personal Reflection:

1. Review the "Principles of HopeFound Living" described in the chapter. To what degree do you genuinely embrace these principles in your life?

2. Specifically consider the significant areas discussed: marriage, parenting, disease, physical suffering, death, career and ministry, and assess to what degree you are living out the "HopeFound Lifestyle" in these areas of your life.

CROSSING THE BRIDGE

The thoughts in this last chapter are written in the hope that some of you reading this book do yearn for the delightful, fulfilling HopeFound lifestyle that I've described, have recognized the need to cross the bridge into HopeFound living, and want direction in that process. If you have not yet entered into eternal relationship with God as His child, that must happen before you go further. HopeFound is a God-inhabited place available only to His children.

My journey across the bridge started with the realization that my make-believe wall of protection was a delusion. That's where it has to start for you. I came to recognize that I unconsciously depended on my indestructible marriage, perfect child, rock-solid career, perfect health, dedicated faith practices, etc., to be planks in a wall of circumstances which would protect me from Paradise-Lost-pain. For me, the event that squashed the delusion of walls of protection was my husband's desertion. Sometimes it is a profound life crisis that breaks through the delusion; sometimes it is just the small, daily disappointments of life that gradually erode away our confidence in our ability to control the circumstances of our lives. However it happens, the journey begins with recognizing the true impotence of delusional walls of protection, and the circumstances that have sub-consciously operated as planks in the wall and soothed us with their false promise of invincibility. As you evaluate whether you are currently residing in HopeFound or in a delusional wall of protection, ask yourself these questions: Have I worked very hard to create and sustain a set of circumstances that I naively believe enables me to program the positive outcomes I want from life? Do I believe that my sincere, driven efforts to construct a set of safe circumstances will be honored by God with His blessing and protection from suffering? Has this quest for comfort been the God that I have worshipped, even more than the true God?

STEP ONE: REALIZE THE DELUSION, RECOGNIZE THE PLANKS

I hope that reading this book has been used by God to awaken you to the deception of believing that you can and must build a wall of protection from the suffering inevitably present here in Paradise Lost. From the beginning of human history Satan, the author of all lies, has so successfully used this lie to distract us from God's greatest purposes for us, and to impel us to wastefully invest massive quantities of the talent, time, energy, and resources God has given us in this meaningless pursuit. Are you ready to quit the delusion?

A helpful process to break down delusional walls of protection is to take them apart plank by plank. What are the circumstances which you have sought passionately, and believe are necessary to provide you with the comfortable, happy life you want? Identify these circumstances specifically and recognize how you have depended on them to protect you from particular kinds of discomfort, based on your personal soul-wound issues. Acknowledge to yourself and to God that your pursuit of these life circumstances has been idolatry, because you have put them above your worship and service to Him. Admit that you cannot protect your heart from all discomforts of human experience in Paradise Lost.

STEP TWO: CROSS THE BRIDGE

Crossing the bridge symbolizes leaving behind the old way and going someplace new. It symbolizes COMMITMENT to leave behind self-absorbed focus on comfortable life circumstances and pursue life from God's perspective. Quitting the impossible task of seeking to control and program your life may initially cause fear and even depression as you LET GO of the fictitious sense of control which has previously been your security, and acknowledge your limitations. Ultimately, however, you will experience a marvelous lightness of heart as you discover that you have been set free from a prison of your own making which no longer owns every ounce of your energy and moment of your days.

Crossing the bridge also symbolizes irreversibility. There must never be a retreat to the old, dysfunctional patterns of self-protective obsession with pleasant life circumstances. See this bridge as "ONE WAY". Commit to vigilantly guard yourself from ever going back over the bridge into meaningless, delusional wall-building.

STEP THREE: BECOME A YIELDED CAST MEMBER TO GOD, THE "SUPREME DIRECTOR"

The essence of HopeFound living lies in recognizing and embracing God's absolute sovereignty and ownership of your life, knowing that you truly exist only to be available to God for His good, trustworthy purposes. Tell God that you are placing yourself completely at His disposal, making available to Him everything you have-time, talents, gifts, resources, energy. Acknowledge absolute commitment to His ways and His purposes as the only thing in life worth living for.

STEP FOUR: TURN PLANKS INTO PROPS

Truly living for God's purposes will require a changed view of the circumstances of your life. Recognize that the circumstances God allows in your life are there to assist in the eternal, spiritual purposes He intends to accomplish through you in them. Bring each of the circumstances which you have identified as false planks in your previous wall-building efforts to God, and yield them to Him as His responsibility, to be used as props on the stage of your life as He pleases, which only provide the background for the action in the drama to be played out there.

STEP FIVE: LET THE DRAMA OF A LIFETIME BEGIN!

Everything is finally in place for the drama of a lifetime to begin! Knowing that you are on this stage, in this place, at this time, to actively participate with God in playing out His plans conceived for you in eternity past is a breath-taking thought! Commit to the lifetime process of getting to know Him better and better, continually being changed by Him, and constantly seeking How he wants to use you in transmitting His love and goodness into your world.

STEP SIX: CELEBRATE THE GOD-MAN COOPERATIVE

As your life in HopeFound continues to unfold, be prepared for the incredible experience of being part of a God-man cooperative! Look upon every moment of everyday as planned by God to cooperatively impact the world and eternity through you! Whether heading for work, or driving to a tennis match, or hanging out laundry, or teaching school, or leading Bible study, or praying with family, or preaching, or whatever else of the infinite number of tasks a day includes, seek and expect God's enablement to do something that matters to Him, and that matters for eternity. Start everyday with the prayer, "Lord, here we are in HopeFound. What are you and I going to do together today?" And keep praying that prayer until the curtain comes down.

Some of you reading this book may already have relocated to HopeFound, though you have not identified it thus. But many reading this book have a choice to make: will I continue to build delusional walls of protection in Paradise Lost or will I relocate to HopeFound? Will I continue to invest my energy and the days of my life in meaningless, self-centered activity which at best gives limited pleasure and fulfillment for a season, and when I am gone will have made not even a tiny ripple of effect on the glorious shores of eternity? Or will I claim God's eternal working in me as my highest calling in life, yielding my quest for comfortable life circumstances and emotional ease to His sovereign control, knowing that as I willingly align with His awesome purposes for my life, whatever He chooses to do with me and through me will break upon the glorious shores of eternity with resounding, God-pleasing impact throughout the eons of eternal time?

Seems like a pretty obvious decision to me. What is holding you up? One thing's for sure, it's not those delusional walls of protection. We all know they don't exist. Not here in Paradise Lost...

For Personal Reflection:

1. The chapter asks these questions: "Have I worked very hard to create and sustain a set of circumstances that I naively believe enables me to program the positive outcomes I want from life? Do I believe that my sincere, driven efforts to construct a set of safe circumstances will be honored by God with His blessing and protection from suffering? Has this quest for comfort been the God that I have worshipped, even more than the true God?" If your answer to these questions is "yes," are you willing to cross the bridge and relocate to HopeFound?

2 IF so, prayerfully follow the steps outlined to bring you to that place of surrender and exciting purpose and peace.

3. Begin today to acknowledge to God everyday your choice to live in HopeFound and your availability to Him to fulfill His plans written for you for this day.

APPENDIX A
EXAMPLES OF
INTERNALIZED
ASSUMPTIONS AND CORE
BELIEFS

- I'm powerless. I'm a victim of outside circumstances.
- If I take a risk, I'll fail. If I fail, others will reject me.
- My feelings and needs are unimportant.
- I should always look good and act nice no matter how I feel.
- I have to make everyone happy all the time.
- I can never be safe in this world.
- People I trust will hurt and disappoint me . Don't trust.
- I should never feel negative emotions like anger, sadness, fear, or jealousy.
- I'm responsible for other people's emotions.
- If I don't want anything, I won't be disappointed.

- Other people's needs are more important than mine.
- I have to be perfect to be accepted/loved.
- I am unlovable or unlikable.
- I am inferior and/or inadequate
- I am insignificant and/or worthless

Breinigsville, PA USA
14 December 2009
229188BV00001B/5/A